Make Me

a memoir
by
lisa stathoplos

Book design and cover art
by michael crockett

For my original family, Mom, Dad, Karen and Mark
and my children, Gelsey and Luke, and for their dad, Todd.
And, for michael.

Mostly, for Mom, my champion and my foil.
Juliette Therese Laferriere Stathoplos
1930 - 2020

Introduction

I dreamt this book. A memory popped into my brain one night - a long ago remembrance of an unpleasant interaction with two radiologists. And then, more stories came. Chapters came to me while sleeping or while lying awake in a fugue state and I woke up and wrote them down. I guess my subconscious had some stuff to say.

Like memory, the timeline of these stories jumps around. I am thinking of one thing that leads to something else that is quite another. I weighed each memory, though, to estimate if it would help to illuminate who I am and how I became "me".

I never intended to write a book. Certainly not a memoir. We had only recently moved to the Belfast area to teach. But, during the 2020 lockdown for Covid-19, schools closed and I was teaching remotely. I had some time on my hands. I began an online writing class. I could have told lots more stories of the events and circumstances of my life that "made me", but these memories are enough. They encompass my first thirty-two years only - before the births of my children. That would be a whole other book that I am not ready to write. Something would really have to MAKE ME.

lisa stathoplos
November, 2020

"Love is the key we must turn
Truth is the flame we must burn
Freedom the lesson we must learn
Do you know what I mean?
Have your eyes really seen?"

Lesley Duncan

Make Me

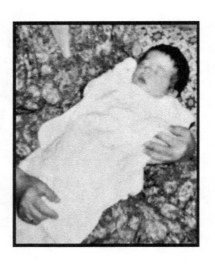

A Space Oddity

WHACK!

It's a....

Wail!

...girl!

Loud sobbing.

Noise, lights, cold, wet.

Here? Again? In a body?

Soul sob.

Rubbing, stroking, warm hands hold my head and bottom.

Congratulations!

Wail.

Some are like this, Juliette; it will pass in time.

Ow. Wailing.

I don't feel good. I am uncomfortable here!

Wet. Sticky. Pointy pain.

Help me! HELP ME!!!

Mom rocks me. Dad walks me.

No, that's not it!

I'm on my stomach now. Warm hand rubbing my back.

Mom sings.

Too ra loo ra loo ra.

I sleep. For a minute.
I wake up.
I'm still HERE?
Wail.
I am a few months old.

Stop being so moody. Stop rocking. Don't be so emotional. Stop kicking your leg. Don't sulk.

I guess sulking is not smiling. Or is it scowling? I scowl.
I sulk all the time; I am good at it. Why would anyone do anything else? I don't know why the world feels uncomfortable.

Uncle Lionel: Hey, Lizza Pizza, smile!
Uncle Joel: She's gonna rock that chair right over!
Aunt Florice: Talk to me, why won't you talk to me?

Stop telling me to "come over here". Why won't you all leave me ALONE?!

Kind loving people like my parents demand I be something I am not. Feel something I cannot: ease.
They are happy and fine. Very loving. Everything was great when it was just the three of them. My big sister, Karen, Mom and Dad. They bonded.

What on earth is wrong with this child?

I want to crawl out of this human skin.
I discover rocking helps. Rocking while humming in a monotone really helps.

Stop doing that!

Mom goes wild when I do this. She thinks I am literally retarded.

Stop doing what?

I know what.

I kick my leg instead. I kick when sitting and I really need to kick myself to sleep. Mom thinks this will cause my eventual death by exhaustion. She lifts my leg into bed and hushes me goodnight.

An eternity passes and the patience of Job pales in comparison before she reaches my bedroom door and pulls it to not quite shut.

Goodnight, Lisa.

Awwwww......finally!
Flooding relief. My leg does what it needs to do.

I see what they see in pictures of myself. The Easter family photo in the hallway of my Yaya and Papou's house in Manchester where I am glowering at the floor standing next to my sister in our predictably matching hot pink dresses with the pale pink bows, my Beatle's bob a bit mussed. I hate dresses. I hate cameras. Drag out your little brick-colored Kodak Brownie and I would just as soon bite you.

Stop telling me to smile.

I can't wait until I am old enough to swear. The F word is gonna be my best friend.

This world. What a fucking nightmare.

Losing My Religion

The Catholic church is a big help.

Midnight Mass in St. Patrick's Cathedral, Bellows Falls, Vermont, my birthplace, just over the New Hampshire state line from Walpole, N.H. where we live. Vatican II has finally been passed by a bunch of grown men who think it's normal to all wear the same scarlet robes and weird hats and no girls allowed in over there at Vatican City. As kids we have no idea what the hell Vatican II is but, clearly, it is a big freakin' deal! So, they did something behind all those walls and the rote Latin my sister and I, little brother and Mom have droned our learned responses to for like, ten years in my case, is in English. The whole damn mass is in English.

Whoa. THIS is what the old man in the pulpit with the interchangeable green, purple, blue or red robes - I guess expressing his various fashion whims each Sunday - has been pounding into us for years?! The metallic purple is my favorite.

We sit in our usual pew order: Mark on Mom's right, Karen to her left and me beside Karen. Dad lucks out. No church for him. Contract agreed upon with Mom before marriage. He's Greek Orthodox. Mom is French Catholic. However, they are ALWAYS a United Front.

In the middle of a stretch of Lord Have Mercys and Christ Have Mercys, I casually rip off the top of my right thumbnail just down to the point of not bleeding. We have been kneeling for like another eternity. I lean toward my sister and extend my newly denuded thumb right under her chin. She glances down.

Baldy.
I whisper with glee.

We stop breathing, we bite our cheeks and shake so hard with repressed gales of giggles and the desire to screech out loud, the kneeler and the entire pew is quaking. We are dying inside at the hilarity of it all, stupid and silly as it is. Tears roll down my face and Karen's is completely scrunched up and bright red.
The priest booms on.

I AM THE WORM!

First time not in Latin.

I AM THE WORM!

I buckle forward grabbing my sister's thigh; she convulses and a small shriek escapes her lips. Our faces are contorted beyond recognition; we are going to explode.

He won't stop. Echoing through the vaulted ceiling:

There will be retribution, Agnes Dei, holy, holy, holy, Lamb of God, take away the sins of the world and all of you have inherited original sin!

I tell a pretty good combo of original sins every week - mostly venial, so forgivable, that get me the hell out of the claustrophobic confessional. But I flirt with tossing in a mortal one every now and then just to keep the priest on his toes. This week I'm gonna try out "coveting my neighbor's wife". I have no idea what that means but it oughta jolt Father Kelly out of his confessional daze.

Yes!
Five Hail Marys and six Acts of Contrition are my Get Out of Jail Free cards this week. Hallafuckinglujiah.

My sister and I continue to shake uncontrollably. Mom shoots one dark look to her left followed by a sharp, quick pain in my wrist where her pinch mark is left.

At last, the best signal Mass is about to end: Communion time! I skulk back from the altar to our pew and force down the tasteless, disgusting wafer. Great. It's stuck halfway down my throat. At least it's predictable. I stifle a small smile at Karen. Laughing in church is endlessly entertaining. Church is the best place to laugh because the rule is, you can't. Ain't nothing funny about Catholic church.

Jesus Christ.

We trudge through the parking lot in the snow and get into the old grey Chevy station wagon. Mom's jaw is set. I'm a dead man walking. It was still worth it.

Catholic Church has me well-trained in defiance. In a picture of my First Communion I look completely dorky in my puffy white dress with the stupid headband crown and veil. At least I'm smiling. Good lord, why?

The CC loves weird rites of passage; I'm guessing those guys in the red robes dream them up while they fantasize about being the next pope. I'm thirteen. It's time for Confirmation. Have they been unaware of me?

It's a magical time for me and Mom. We cannot be alone in the same room together for more than five minutes before I storm off. We don't yell at each other; we freeze each other out. Ours is an epic Cold War happening right on Webhannet Drive, Wells Beach, Maine. She's adamant, though. I WILL be confirmed.

God.

I'm not sure if Mom really buys all this Catholic stuff or if it is just so rotely ingrained in her French upbringing that she doesn't want to upset the apple cart - or take any bad apples. Every woman on earth knows Eve was framed.

We're packed like sardines with legs in the wooden pews of the raised choir section of St. Mary's church in Wells Beach. Sister Anne is in charge of our big transition and leads us through the requirements for Confirmation in weekly class. I confirm my abject contempt.

You must choose a new name- a saint's name.

You've gotta be kidding? I don't know any saints. Pretty sure beatification isn't in my future either - wait five years for your day in eternity? prove two miracles? document heroic acts?! Too many hoops, man.

Sister Anne drills a hole in me with her eyes.

Okay, okay. The big star saints get listed during mass every Sunday. Sister Anne frowns deeply at me.

Umm..... Ignatius!

I always liked that name.

You will be Marie.

What the hell?! Why can't I be Ignatius?! I hate this woman. What a control freak! I found out years later that Ignatius was a male saint. Who knew? Ignatius is a kick ass girl's name. I wasn't even trying to piss that nun off but, in my ignorance, did anyway. Good job.

There's a picture of Mom and me from this day standing in front of the church. I'm in my long white robe with the red collar, my sun streaked blonde and untrimmed hair painfully tamed at last - I haven't brushed it for, like, ten years - blowing slightly in the breeze. Looking at the camera I positively glower. Mom looks like she's on death row. Like I said, it was magical.

I do have a spiritual life. Kind of. I mean, I feel like there is something like love that is the one true thing and we all just become one with the universe when we die or at least that would be nice. Sometimes I get a lump in my throat when

I think about the concept of infinity; it drives me near madness if I dwell on it. I try not to dwell on it. But an old white guy who lives up in the sky who was dreamed up by a whole buncha white guys who tell us this Big Old White Guy will welcome us into his Forever Hippie Garden as long as we don't act like assholes and make sure to say He's The One? Oh, and, plus, he sent his only son - not a daughter, they don't count in the CC - to die for us (I always wondered why? Why that? I don't get it.) so we can lounge in his gated community ever after? Hard for me to swallow. Sometimes when the world seems so dark and mean and full of horrors, I lie awake and think this thing:

I could be a better God than you.

I get so mad at a God who would create a world with so much pain for all living creatures that I want to scream. Or, if we are supposed to come here to learn some crazy eternal lesson that we contracted to learn before we got here and then He/She/It makes it so we don't remember the contract and are just set up for failure? That sucks, too.

I call FOUL!!!!! I can make up a better world than this!

I get it. It's got all this beauty and whatnot but only with unimaginable pain and suffering guaranteed. And, at the end? You get to DIE!

Are you SERIOUSLY SERIOUS?!!!! What kind of twisted plan is this??!!!!! Hello? God???!! God.

Pretty sure whenever I think this I am damned to hell for all eternity; they're already at work on another circle. I see myself sliding reluctantly down an imagined steel silo, the neon "Abandon All Hope" sign blinking its caution at the bottom, with my arms and legs splayed and skidding, squeaking against the sleek sides while looking up the whole time screaming:

And ANOTHER thing!!!

I can also see the bolt of lightning shooting out of a cloud killing me instantly when I think this. Guess the fact that hasn't happened yet is a freakin' miracle.

If I'm wrong, God? Just hand me a couple more Our Fathers and we'll call it good, okay?

Voices In My Head

When you drive up to the house it will be on fire but, it's okay, everyone is in the car.

Shut UP!

We are driving back from Manchester where we visited my Greek grandparents and the voice in my head is getting louder. It's really freaking annoying. This is a thing that happens to me; I get feelings or thoughts and they turn out to be true. My Yaya has this in spades. She "sees" things in the future with astonishing accuracy. She saw my dad's ship, the U.S.S. Borie, the last ship to be hit by a Japanese kamikaze plane in WWII, in flames with dead men on deck and in the water. Three days later the Navy told her about it. Told her Dad was alive. Three days later. Shitty three days for Yaya I would think. Her clairvoyance is legendary in my family. She's seen a lot of things.

I hate this "ability" in myself. My darkness makes me assume bad things will always happen, so I have been working on pushing this undesirable talent away.

Rounding Webhannet Drive to the seawall, I see a shroud of thick, black smoke enveloping both of our houses - the summer cottage we rent out and our inn. Flames are shooting out of the cottage's roof. My parents are in shock and Karen and Mark are yelling. I am weirdly calm. The voice told me already. We are all in the car and it is just a house. I do not freak out.

It turns out it really is okay because neither house is on fire. The couple renting our cottage had an enormous bonfire in the huge fireplace and the chimney caught. Fortunately, it burned itself out with my dad's help. He removed the flaming logs. He's a high school chemistry and physics teacher. I'm thinking the couple renting the cottage got a schooling they won't soon forget.

Other times, these thoughts and feelings are more vague but the reliability of their accuracy is unnerving. I don't wanna know about things before they happen; what's happening right now is enough.

I Discover Radium

Slam. Bam. No thank you ma'am. My mother's frosty glare threatens petrification of her targets. She's the best at frosty glares. I don't recommend going head-to-head with her. Two female radiologists are clearly pissed off that we have the audacity to show up at 3:50 PM, ten minutes before their apparent quitting time. Thing One Radiologist and Thing Two Radiologist are having none of Dr. Chansons' orders to check the status of my double S curvature of the spine. As a result of which, my parents and I will dutifully trek down to One Emerson Square, Boston Children's Hospital in our '69 Blue Saab bug where the bespectacled and respected Dr. Peter Zagreb, orthopedic surgeon of Egyptian descent, will ceremoniously extract the films from their huge manila envelope and with the now so familiar "thwap" of reflexive rubber, smack them one after the other onto his magically lit screen, discern my progress and recommend further treatment.

Back in York, the two Put-upons humph and sigh and then direct me to the darkened and sterile X-ray room where I obediently disrobe from the waist up and don the obligatory paper gown. Bam. Door slams back open.

You ready?

Ready for what?, I think. Ready to find out the curves have now altered another barely discernible fraction of some measurement?

I just want the pain to stop. I hate this. Slam. Rapid breath intake. Bony chest pressed up against the backlit square with two lines bisecting like a taunting geometric puzzle. Cold. Cold. Cold.

Don't move. Hold your breath. Bzzzzt. Okay. Breathe. Relax. Turn to your left. Radiologist Two sighs.

Icy hands shove me, manhandle my left shoulder down and against the geometric figure. Presses it down again. Sighs.

Move forward. Not that much. You have to hold still.

No shit.

I casually calculate the number of rads my slender frame has absorbed in the bowels of hospitals such as this in the past almost two years. Thanks, Madame Curie.

Okay, good. Don't move. Hold your breath. Bzzzt.

Repeat the entire sequence on the right side.

Okay. Don't get dressed. Wait here. I have to check the pictures.

She's a friggin' heartbeat away from Neils Bohr deconstructing the atom. I slump on cold steel.

Thing One Radiologist is back.

Okay. Get dressed. You can go.

Fuck you. In my head only. I am fourteen.

I go back and meet Mom in the waiting room. Who. Is. Seething.

Who is your immediate supervisor?

Thing One barely registers Mom's inquiry. Their ultimate supervisor would be John Rogers, hospital administrator. I knew Mom knew him and I knew she would talk to him, a kind man long in the job from what I gather who apparently has some knowledge of how and how not to run a small hospital. Whatever Mom said in her meeting that I was not a part of seems to have resulted in my never running into those two particular radiologists in my years to come of radium-fueled photographs taken at York.

So now, physical therapy and multiple X-rays have become my new world. One good thing: I absolutely adore my physical therapist, Paulette Gendron- so much so, I decide I am going to become one myself.

I wonder if math is involved?

I do get to work alongside her every Saturday morning as she puts her geriatric patients through their paces. I help Mrs. Jackson and then Mr. Cooper, both advanced octogenarians, on the parallel bars walk as they try to recover from whatever needs recovering from. From the look of them, a lot. Paulette tells me it is a joy to work with someone as young and motivated as me because she can watch the progress weekly. I beam. Progress for most of her patients, I guess, is in their rearview. I love being with Paulette. I have her for years but then she either retired or moved on and I have others. None made me as happy as she did.

I'm well into my era of physical therapist appointments thrice weekly and looking forward to years of spinal correction when I decide it's a good time to stop eating.

Old Milwaukee Brace

Hey, Flatso! Loud, calling me from the back of the bus. Hey, Flat and ugly! Are you bored? Cuz ya look like a board! Ha, ha, ha!

End of friggin' school for the day and, oh joy, the ride home on the beach kids' bus - all nine of us. And, neat, the two four-foot dipshits from my class with a two-digit combined IQ - my own personal schoolyard dumbasses - are at it again.

Hey, flatso! You're ugly! You're flat AND ugly!
Is there no limit to their genius? Bus pulling out at last - Route One to Mile Road and across the marsh and - Atlantic Avenue? Really?! We're going all the way down to the harbor for one new kid? Ugh. The creative chants continue.

Flat and ugly, flat and ugly, flat and ugly. Ha, ha, ha!

Will they never tire of yelling what I already know? I just sit and stare dully through my window prison at the clutter of empty seasonal cottages whizzing by.

In my head I say:

Hey, fuckers! I know I'm not pretty and I look like a boy, you playground moron creeps - I'm a tomboy, shitforbrains! Wanna know what I do after school? 400 fucking reps of upper and lower body spinal work. It only takes about an hour and a half out of every single day but I could take both of you with one well-placed kick with an enviably toned leg before you croak out your next moronic witticism!

At last, the seawall and open air and the endless moving blue vista that is the ocean and my home. A wall of reenergizing sea air engulfs me as I mercifully step off the number 28 and wave to our garrulous bus driver, Rick Bowen. Yeah, right. His monosyllabic barks and rude manner have no doubt scarred hundreds of kids before me. After seven years of living in Maine I still wonder if he remembers my friggin' stop. Big sign saying Fisherman's Cove Inn oughta be a dead giveaway but I don't think he was at the top of his class.

Our house is a haven even if Mom and I fight a lot. It is a good home and I know it even as I often want to flee it. Warm smell of granny stove and the tea kettle chattering with its large contents of boiling water. Cookies baking or soup stewing and the comforting smell of woodsmoke. I don't hang out in it though. Time to head upstairs, chuck my shit into my freezing room and begin my routine. The routine I adhere to with a monk's fervor to stave off the horrendous possibility of a full body Milwaukee Brace or spinal surgery.

Yeah, Milwaukee. Shit, up to now, I thought they only made beer.

At my very first visit with Dr. Zagreb, he explains to me and my horrified parents in nail-biting detail exactly what my serpentine spine is doing to my internal organs and why it is causing incessant pain. In a nutshell, my spine is squeezing all of my gastrointestinal tract - in my case, a real marvel of human genetics - together with no room to function normally. Hence, pain. He then describes options. Option A: intensive physical therapy, possibly entailing years of hard labor to correct curves, Option B: the mysterious but soon to be illuminated Milwaukee Brace or Option C, and last chance at help: spinal surgery.

Mom gasps. Kidding. Mom never gasps; she stuffs all her anxiety and masks it with incredibly piercing and knowledgeable questions. Mom reads a little.

Okay, wow. Exercises seem fine but, what the hell is a Milwaukee Brace? Handily, there is one on a skeletal model right in Dr. Zagreb's office/showroom. It is a medieval contraption of leather and metal that cups the chin and the neck and fastens the entire upper torso in a kind of Dark Ages straitjacket. Future Inquisitors might want to swap out the thumbscrews. With this possibility, the bus ride's looking better every day.

There are probably many in your school who wear these! exclaims Dr. Zagreb exuberantly in his warm Egyptian lilt, clearly unaware of rural areas outside of Greater Boston.

No!!!! There are exactly ZERO fucking kids wearing these nightmarish contraptions in my Wells, Maine high school with a potential graduating class of about 80!

I play basketball and run track, for Christ's sake - there is no FUCKING way I am going to wear that thing; I will deal with the pain!

So, intensive physical therapy it is. No change in three months and I'm getting put on the rack. Talk about motivation. Mom and Dad are on board for whatever it takes to stop the pain but, for now, seem pleased with my less invasive attempt. Spinal surgery is an absolute last resort.

So, yeah, daily standing sets, hanging sets, prone sets, side sets, wall sets and now to sit sets- all in the hallway between my brother's room and mine. Eyeing my parent's transportable full-length mirror as I sit, spine flattened to the wall, arms pushed back into it, I compress my two scapulae toward my spinal column and slowly force my arms outward resisting the push always and being certain that my left shoulder reflection stays in line with my right.

Whoa. My cheeks look chubby today. When the hell did that happen? Come to think of it, my jeans don't feel as loose as always. Okay, gross. Gotta fix this.

I eat all the time. That's it! I never overeat - have never even understood what people mean when they say they are stuffed - but I snack all day while running in and out. Always have. I resolve to eat only my three meals a day. No snacking.

Ta da! Two or three weeks in and no more fat cheeks, jeans feeling normal, whatever that is, getting a bit too baggy even and, pretty soon, it warrants a rare trip to Ames Department Store with Mom to change sizes.

I never looked at scales much before but now, my parents' bathroom scales lure me in daily. Okay. Started at around 130 and now down to 120. Excellent. Just need to keep up the good work. Meals start getting smaller or skipped altogether when possible. And then, something happens that makes skipping supper, the meal my family always eats together, possible.

Around January when I turn seventeen, my creative writing teacher corners me after class in the sun-soaked west wing of Wells High School and says this lunatic thing.

I'd like you to try out for the school play.

I'm wearing this new red and white sheath dress Mom got me for Christmas from Sawyer Mills in Dover and, with my gold hooped pierced earrings, I guess I feel pretty great for like, the first time ever, but, really?

Okay.

Shit. Try out? Like, how? Try out thinking anyone would want to watch me onstage? Crap. How do I get outta this?!

I must confess here that I really like this teacher, and love her class and I know she likes my writing but it all seems hard to believe.

Last summer, though, between sophomore and junior year, I made a big decision that changed my life. Up until then I was just a jeans and frayed jean jacket frumpy closet reefer girl who was somehow accepted by the most popular kids with whom I didn't really belong. I do have my beach kid friend, Gem. She's a year younger than me, though, and we are kind of growing apart.

But, summers. Summers were when I had a real tribe. Around August fourth every year, the Cosettis and the Landons from Acton and Leominster Mass came up and rented the Magnolia cottage down the street from me for three straight weeks. With them and our friend Cindy Jameson from Holderness, NH who stayed all summer in the Wild Wave, a few of my beach friends and I became thick as thieves. When I was with my summer friends, I could be myself. I even fell in love for the first time with Danny Cosetti and he loved me back. It was absolutely thrilling. We prowled Wells Beach and the Casino area, just an arcade and movie theatre, smoked cigarettes and pot, swam in

Fisherman's Cove, and endlessly played Neil Young's HARVEST and Zep's ZOSO. Mike Cosetti got a hold of a new Boston band's album that WRKO Boston was playing all the time and it blew our minds so DREAM ON by Aerosmith regularly blared from the summer porch at the Cosettis. In summer, I could just be me - something I never felt at school. So, the decision was: go back to school in the fall and be the real, authentic me. And I did. What happened, weirdly, is everyone accepted me - the jocks, the stoners, the nerds, the artists - everyone. Strange times.

I've added lipstick to my look. Orange is nice and Mom has it and wears it. I like it. I am buying lipstick now and I am wearing it always. Mascara, too. I guess it makes me look like someone she wants in the play. I know she will realize her horrible mistake but, feeling weirdly brave, I go to the tryouts. I get the lead. Wow.

First rehearsal, major realization. I feel completely at home here. Lisa disappears here. I could just live here. And, this is perfect because now I am at play practice every school night and, boy, do I have this not eating thing mastered so there can be more plays after this. Barely a cup of homemade granola in the morning, skip lunch and, if I have to be home at dinner and not at play practice, which is rare now, just push food around on my plate, give some to the two cats at my feet and shove the rest in a napkin to put in the trash while doing dishes. Easy-peasy.

115! Yes! Can't stop now. If I stop, I will get fat.

Lisa, I've taken in this gown twice now. Are you eating enough, honey?

Looks of consternation are exchanged by the clearly jealous Home Ec teacher/Costume Designer and my Creative Writing teacher/Director.

This is so fucked up. They are messing with my head. I am friggin' fat. Whoa. When did that shift happen? How did that shift happen? Wasn't I just trimming down slightly, halting the flesh gain that would have invariably left me fat? I am now afraid to be fat. I am now afraid of food. This is good. This is what needed to happen.

Lisa, can I talk to you?

My Psych teacher captures me in the hallway by Rothoff's room.

Jesus. She's part of it. And, I kinda liked her 'til now even if she and her husband hang out with my parents sometimes, which is always complicated. She drives a slick silver Toyota Celica, wears kinda groovy pants at school - not a lot of female teachers do that. It's the early seventies.

Leave me alone! What do these people want from me?! I'm fine. I have the lead in the school play, am the sixth man on our winning basketball team now headed to the States, have mostly A's and B's and I weigh around, what? 110 pounds? Back off!
I politely say:

Oh, yeah, no, I'm fine. I get hot lunches now.

Liar. No one needs to know I've been living on one boiled egg a day for a while now. That is IT! It's great. I haven't had a period in months but, hey, don't knock the bonuses!

Wells High School gym. THE GREAT SEBASTIANS by Lindsey and Crouse going up in a week. Designer and Director gang up. Costumes have been altered for the third? fourth time?

We're worried, honey.

Uh, huh. Yup. Okay. I will. Sure.

Polite as heck to their faces but, ohmygod, can they not SEE?! I am not too thin; I am barely acceptable to myself in any lurking mirror and, what's worse, if I don't keep to this diet I will explode into a giant, fat, disgusting blob! I know it is a conspiracy; I know they are seriously jealous or some weird thing. I only need to continue to nod and acquiesce yet never waver from my one true goal: eat close to nothing.

Then, around Easter, my brother, Mark, hops through the kitchen where I rock by the granny stove cranking LEVON from Elton John's MADMAN ACROSS THE WATER on my headset and he's got a whole jar full of Good n' Fruity. For the first time in nine months, I desperately want something sweet.

Can I have some?

He's feeling generous. Dumps a handful.

More?

More??!!! An alien is inhabiting my brother's body. Probably near to a cup I manage. So sweet, so good. I practically swallow them whole. I start vomiting around two AM. Then, I get really sick and pass out. Everything coming out both ends. Mom gets me to the shower before a trip to the ER. In the shower, feeling very unsteady, I look down at my body for the first time in months. I can see every rib; my hip bones look like something in a museum. My formerly thick long hair is just plain falling out in my hands.

For the first time, I think: I look like shit.

And I'm scared. I am almost five feet, nine inches tall. This morning the scales read 105 pounds.

Can't remember much in the ER - I guess tests and stuff; they like to do tests. But I remember one thing that, even at the time, I knew I would never forget. Attending physician, Dr. Dodge, standing near the examining table and looking down at me where I sit feeling miserable says:

You have two options: you can either eat, or you can die.

Memorable. A literal "click" went off in my head as if my life force had been shut off for a while and the switch just got thrown again. I want to go home and eat a hamburger or ten. Of course, that is not possible. My body has to relearn to accept food, so, even though I slowly get better and begin to eat again, I still hate my body; it needs constant correction. The other thing is, it really hasn't liked me that much since I was about eleven when my first swing through medical testing began. See, my intestines never really worked right and they were kind of always mixed up in the whole spinal/gastrointestinal thing that mystified my doctors so. I really hate stumping the medical establishment all the time, what with all their fun tests and whatnot; although, I never helped much because I either didn't understand Dr. Sanjay with his vowel-rich East Indian accent or, I just clammed up about symptoms too embarrassing to admit to. In short, I was the perfect candidate for the inimitable and endlessly irritating Irritable Bowel Syndrome diagnosis. Meaning, basically, we have no idea what is wrong with you but here's a diagnosis to last a lifetime.

I guess Celiac disease never crossed their minds.

Burn Down The Mission

I'm standing amidst a pile of giant pink swans swimming in a black sea while holding the roller and looking up at Mom.

Shitadamn!

Her signature swear. She's on the top rung of the ladder in Apartment 3 of Fisherman's Cove Inn and she just whacked her head on the ceiling. Snapping her fingers.

Is the next sheet ready?

Hello. I'm right here!

I pass her the top edge of the sticky wallpaper - this one in soft hues of yellow and orange - I've just plastered thick paste all over. It predictably folds onto itself about three quarters of the way down the length and sticks.

Fucking piece of crap!!!!

I can only say this inside my head. Mom does not tolerate any swears - except the few she says - and NEVER EVER the F word.

Wallpapering is a task Mom and I like doing together. Detente happens. The swans are oblivious. Giant shreds of them lie all over the floor. Their time has come and whoever chose the ghastly black paper they were trapped in for God knows how many years is likely long gone along with their dubious decorating style. I kick a clump of them out of the way as I wade over to help Mom align the tiny carnations and daisies accurately from ceiling to floor and roll out the wrinkles with my handy tool from Aubuchon hardware.

We have wallpapered many, many rooms, Mom and I. This is a place where we connect. We share an aesthetic for design and art and making a space homey. Which is weird since I am always thinking of running away from home but that is because my parents are very strict.

Sometimes Uncle Joel, a professional house painter and paperer, helps us. Mom is always annoyed with the paper, Joel always makes her laugh and both Mom and I are always thrilled with the results when the newly hung paper completely alters a room.

One time I was with Mom in one of our local haunts for both upholstery material and wallpaper, Bosal Foam, on Route One in Scarborough, and Mom sees a roll of contact paper that catches her eye.

Ohmygod! That would look great in the kitchen!

I eye it and I can see it. The orange cantaloupes, green cabbages and magenta beets in squares of yellows and green could look amazing next to our newly painted chocolate brown cupboards. But, CONTACT paper? I am very familiar with working with this tool of the devil; I have had to line many drawers in our new inn with it. Howling swears I did not know I knew is my most vivid memory of the task. She snaps up five or six rolls.

We choose a cool October evening for the project. Handily, Uncle Joel and beloved cousins Susie, Linda and Amy are staying with us for the weekend. We are all excited to begin - right after supper. Stupid time to start. It does not disappoint. It is utterly infuriating to work with. Actually, it cannot be worked with; it sticks to everything that so much as exists near it, folds onto itself in ways that would shame real wallpaper and is nearly impossible to unstick once stuck.

Juliette!

Joel in his French singsong.

What?!

I can't work with this! Are you really sure you like this?

Yes, yes!

Passes him a length of bright cabbages and beets that handily sticks to the ladder.

Linda and I are cutters and passers. We are all "matchers" - finding where in the roll the next cantaloupe half meets its reflective twin. We work on into the night. The kitchen is big and there's a lot of wall space in between cupboards. Occasional swears and sighing aside, we are an amiable group enjoying a night's work. Joel rolls out the last stubborn wrinkle on the final wall. All of us step back to admire our work. We wait for Mom to do what she does: leave the room and then walk back in to see its effect. The walls are very nearly vibrating in electric and dizzying colour.

OHMYGODWENEEDTOTAKETHATALLDOWN!!!!!!!

We are all stunned. But I know she is right. The walls scream at you, demand you see only them - now and in your night terrors forever - such is the effect of too much bright contact paper on too much wall.

We begin the awful, awful task of peeling the wretched contact paper off the wall. Someone starts to giggle and Mom starts to laugh. She has a great laugh. An infectious, joyful laugh. She cannot stop. Soon we are a mass of frenzied people madly ripping great strips of color from the walls while laughing hysterically. We cannot stop. It is an epic failure that leaves us epically amused. Eventually, I help Mom paper the kitchen with a sweet and calming lemon yellow print that enhances the kitchen's natural charm. But I won't soon forget those neon cabbages and beets. Man, wallpapering is freakin' annoying. I'll probably paint from here on.

Blind Faith

The pouring rain is putting a real damper on this whole running away from home thing.

I'm sitting in the Bel Aire Diner on Route One somewhere outside of Saugus, Mass waiting for my summertime boyfriend, Danny, to show up and take me away. To where? I haven't quite figured that part out - we're both still in high school. A couple of hours ago I was nervously shifting my feet at the counter of Moulton's store in Wells buying my first Greyhound bus ticket to Boston after Mom and I had another blowout over my latest restrictions. I've got the most backward parents in the friggin' universe, that is for sure. Most Backward Parent Award SEWN up for all time!

Running away always seemed inevitable. Now it's seeming like a crappy idea; I have no money, no plan and I'm hungry and my anger of just hours ago has cooled some. When Danny arrives in his Dad's old Ford Fairmont, talking me out of this isn't too hard. He drives me back to Maine. At least I get to see him. That never happens after August. Maybe that's all I wanted. I really don't know what I want except some elusive thing I call freedom. And to already be grown up and on my own. I do not know how not ready I am for that; I just want out from under my parents' thumbs. They are so suffocatingly strict that, by the time we get to my house at the seawall, I don't think they even knew I was gone.

People Suck

What the...?

Blinking up at the cloudy sky I can feel the grit of the pavement on my back; my left arm and leg are twisted under me. Blue metal trash barrels with OPW - Ogunquit Public Works - lie flung nearby. Ugh, they stink.

Where's my bike?
A hand reaches down and pulls me to sitting. A small crowd is standing around. Why do I feel embarrassed?

Are you okay? That guy just came out of nowhere!

Yeah, yeah. I'm okay. My bike.....?

Another person wheels it over; everything is kind of a blur. I get up. My ankle is messed up and there's a wicked scrape full of dirt bleeding on my calf and on my elbow, too. I look at my yellow Schwinn. The handlebars are torqued. Fuckin A! My new bike! I guess I didn't hit my head. Ha, ha! Feeling around, no blood there. It's the 1970s; there's no such thing as routine helmet wearing. All my money has to go to college; I can't afford a new bike.

You sure you're okay? Do you need a ride?

No, no, thanks, I'm okay.
I limp walk my bike to the red and white phone booth by the Gulf station. My ankle feels like shit. What a fucking asshole! Just blew off the three-way

intersection in the center of town packed with summer traffic and going god knows what, slams me and my bike into the barrels and takes off? People suck.

In my pocket are a few tips from my tour guide job aboard the lobster boat The Plain Jane out of Perkins Cove; I find that one thin dime.

Hi, Dad?

My voice is shaky; I do NOT want to cry.

I think I need a ride. My bike is messed up.

Dad's always calm. I guess being a WWII Navy Medic aboard a destroyer in the Pacific Theater helps.

Lizzie? Where are you?

He calls me Lizzie. Huh. He's worried.

This daily fourteen mile round trip I make from Webhannet Drive to Bourne Avenue then Route one to Shore Road is nothing new; I've done it to get to work every summer for years. One jerk won't stop me.

Dad fixes my bike.

Thanks, Dad.

But, he gives me a ride to The Cove for about a week or so while my sprained ankle heals. We don't say much on these early morning and late evening rides but Dad always lets me pick the radio station. Right now Ian Anderson is LIVING IN THE PAST with Jethro Tull. Dad really likes Tull. I like these rides with Dad.

Early morning in The Cove.

Have you loaded the salt water tank yet?

The fuck you think I'm doing, Mean Marlene? My affectionate name for the wife of the captain, Kurt Fowler. She's walking alongside me as I lug two 5-gallon buckets filled with seawater - one in each hand - from her restaurant, The Fisherman's Hub across from the Perkins Cove footbridge, to the town dock about 500 yards away to his boat named, as local legend has it, for his first beloved wife, The Plain Jane. I am limping something fierce. She's oblivious.

You are late; this should have been done by eight o'clock.

Really? Wow, thanks for that completely insensitive reminder! I don't know if you wear those friggin' Aviators to look cool or to mask recent blindness but, if you haven't noticed, I just got nailed by a car two days ago and my ankle's not quite right and, by the fucking way, I have never been late and I work hard at this job for nine hours daily and, what the fuck is it that YOU do anyway?

She's about two hundred and fifty years younger than her husband Kurt who I don't get why she's with because he's a piece of friggin' work, too. He thinks he owns not only The Cove but the open ocean beyond it. They are together nonetheless and make quite a pair - him with his scaly green oilskins smelling of rank bait and her in her jodhpurs just back from riding her high horse. She wears straight brown hair plastered against her skull and tied in a tight knot at the nape of her neck for some bizarre reason. She'd be really pretty if she didn't act like such a piece of shit. She thinks my fellow tour guide, Faith, and I are way beneath her.

Get that water in the tank and get back up here and arrange these donuts in baskets. This trip needs to leave in ten minutes.

Yes, ma'am!

We smile with wider than wide smiles. And then we smile some more.

Struggling with our loads and aiming to retain purchase on the ramp to the dock, which is at an almost ninety degree angle at dead low tide, without careening forward, Faith helps me feel better:

Mean Marlene, you nasty machine! Wouldn't wanna be you! "Oh, the bitch, yeah, the bitch, oh, the bitch is back......."

She actually sings this out loud to the entire cove while on her way down the ramp in front of me. I think Elton John would approve. Marlene's nowhere around but I think I will wet my pants while doubling over and skidding off the tar paper at the ramp's bottom.

Mean nasty Marlene!

I'm not working for Mean Marlene on the wrong boat for one more summer.

Tomorrow Never Knows

The inn my mom and dad bought and remodeled themselves is cozy and quaint and filled with antiques Mom finds for ridiculous bargains and with her eye for design, repurposes to fabulous effect. In summer, guests come from all over the place but we have a lot of French Canadians. They are fans of small, pensione type lodgings. Mom's fluent French probably adds to the allure.

My parents stubbornly exploit child labor; my sister and I are expected to work from 8:30 am until 2 pm every day; we begin at age 13. But the Inn is pretty cool and we meet interesting characters. Karen and I wash, dry and hang sheets and towels, scrub bathrooms and kitchenettes, change beds and wash windows. Windows are my specialty; upstairs windows bordering the porch roof and covered in crusty winter salt spray are my exclusive purview. I stand astride a pile of old newspapers with my Windex bottle on the long roof of the front porch and admire the view of the Atlantic all the way to France before attacking Number 6's gritty mess of windows. So weird, but I love this job and I am good at it.

Only Mom or Dad check people in. I wish I could check people in. I want to escort each guest into our spacious living room, rich in earth-colored upholstery and eclectic art, sidle them up to the huge secretary with its myriad cubbies and slots for postcards and envelopes, its fold-out desk and impressive Registrar with signatures from years long before my parents bought this inn. And then, look on as they scribble their names and addresses and license numbers onto the narrow lines. I wish.

Tonight the rain is coming down in sheets and lashing the front windows of Fisherman's Cove Inn. It is a cold June night and we have turned off the VACANCY sign outside; by nine o'clock most guests have already checked in. Suddenly, there is a frantic knocking at the door and Mom answers. A bedraggled but pretty young woman stands, completely drenched, and asks for a room. The only one available is Apartment Three at the top of the stairs - too much money for her and she doesn't want the kitchenette. She just needs a room for the night.

I am lurking by the door to our kitchen watching Mom interact with this girl and I feel there is something very wrong. I'm only fifteen but I get the sense she is afraid or running from something; I have no idea how I know this but I do. I am hoping Mom can give her the apartment at a lower rate that she has enough money for. Mom does. Sensing my presence, Mom asks me to get extra towels and bring them up to Apt. 3.

I am excited. I go to the laundry room hoping the best, most plush towels that are my favorites are clean. They are. Big and thick with a striking black, green and yellow pattern that looks mid-Eastern, I grab two of them, fold them perfectly and, like a sacred offering, take them up the stairs. I knock and she opens her door tentatively, then, smiles when she sees me. Her hair is a mass of long, tight curls now that it's dried some. She's really pretty. I am beguiled. She is standing in front of the enormous mahogany bureau with its massive mirror that came with the inn; I can watch our interaction in it. She thanks me and, this is weird but, I think we recognize a kindred spirit in each other because she tells me her name is Belinda and I tell her mine. And then, we talk for a few minutes - nothing memorable - but the feeling I had that she was in trouble and was glad someone helped her, at least for the night, doesn't go away.

In the morning, she is long gone. I know I will remember her. I know there is something about empathy and a longing to understand other people's very different lives that exists in me and I know that I will use all this someday. I don't know what for.

No Senator's Son

I know there is something not quite right about Gem's mom.
There is a weight in Gem's house that lands on my shoulders every time I walk in the door; I never get used to it. It haunts me.

Gem and I run in through her back door on Ocean Avenue and greet her mom after school. Gonna grab a snack and head out to our hangouts.

Hi, Mrs. Graham!

She smiles vaguely and waves.

She is always in her terry cloth bathrobe and shabby mint-colored fuzzy slippers and she shuffle slides through the kitchen restlessly from one end to the other, window to window, in a kind of skater's waltz with no skates. She looks out each window for a second and continues around her kitchen rink. The TV is always on but she's never watching. She never even sits. I think it's Edge of Night right now. TVs are never on in my house except after dinner and then, with strict rules. The record player is in the living room with the TV; Gem's mom doesn't play any records.

See ya, Mom! Be home in time for chop suey!

Gem always knows what she's having for dinner by the day of the week. It's Tuesday, so.....yeah. And, we're off.

I can't wait 'til after school tomorrow. On Wednesdays Mrs. Graham goes grocery shopping with their neighbor and we have the house to ourselves. I only care because of the music. Rock and roll is everything.

On Wednesdays, we slip into Gem's brother, Stevie's, room, grab some of his albums and crank tunes in the living room. He has every rock album ever made and, plus, he won't mind, he's dead. He died in Vietnam. Gem never told me how. He's just dead. His room is off limits when her mom is home. We can't go in; this is unspoken but I know. The crack left in the door reveals a darkened space with curtains drawn and secrets hidden. I wonder why the door stays shut.

But Wednesdays! Off the bus, I meet Gem at the abandoned swimming pool on Seaview Lane and she hikes with me back down to her house. We go directly to Stevie's room and gently push open the door. It smells kind of stale but kind of like patchouli, too. His room is a little eerie. Everything is left as he left it, untouched - well, except his albums. We've been handling his albums forever like reckless thieves returning to the scene of our crimes. I grew up with John, Paul, George and Ringo living at our house. Like 10 bazillion other humans. But, my taste in music is expanding. Every single great rock band in bookcases that are all organized by group. We grab Joplin's CHEAP THRILLS, The Stones' LET IT BLEED, Cream's DISRAELI GEARS and LED ZEP II. Today, though, we've got something of our own besides SUNSHINE OF YOUR LOVE. Gem saved her weekly allowance for, like, fifty years, and bought the double live album MADE IN JAPAN by Deep Purple.

OHMYGOD!!!!!!!!!!

For her, it's HIGHWAY STAR endlessly and for me it's Ian Gillan, High God of Rock Vocalists, in CHILD IN TIME with his crazy high As? Gs?, or some humanly impossible notes, and, of course, the long and live version of SMOKE ON THE WATER. Sorry, neighborhood of Ocean Avenue!!!!! This album is OUR NEW ANTHEM!

Damn. One hour flies. Gem's mom drives in. Gotta go now.

Get DISRAELI GEARS! Did we take the Stones?

We place each album back in its nest. I glance back as we shut Stevie's door behind us. The American flag on the wall, the India print bed covering, fatigues with multiple patches on the arms, psychedelic peace sign.

Can you see us, Stevie? Thanks for letting us listen to your albums.

C'mon, Lisa!

Gem calls to me from the kitchen.

Coming!

I wonder what it's like to have a brother who died in a war. I wonder what it's like to die at 21. Stevie was a decorated member of the 101st Airborne. Stevie killed himself in Vietnam.

When The Levee Breaks

Lisa!

My Dad's voice, sharp and urgent. He doesn't have a sharp and urgent voice. I wake from a normally fitful sleep and blink my eyes in the dark. Dad never comes to my bedroom. Crash! A wave shudders the entire house. This one obviously cleared the second seawall. Ba DOONG! Slamming splash. Spray from this one hits my bedroom window. Kinda puts some much-needed perspective on Ritter's Algebra quiz tomorrow.

Your mom is making hot cocoa. Get up! We're going downstairs now to have some.

Wow. It's 2 am. This is weird. Is Mom getting high now?

I stumble into the dim hallway upstairs where I meet my sister, Karen, and brother, Mark, looking as bleary-eyed and confused as I am. Dad ushers us toward the asbestos fire door separating the downstairs from the upstairs per OSHA code for inns. The house rattles as another wave smashes into it. Navigating the stairs means traversing the front of the house. Dad nearly pushes us down the hall to the kitchen. I slam open the inner door to the kitchen, primarily in place for privacy in summer and to keep out the freezing cold during the rest of the year. It is January 1972 and the strongest Nor'easter of the season is bearing down on us. Mom smiles benignly at the stove while holding the stirring spoon in a death grip, and asks a bit too cheerily if we'd like cocoa.

Wow. We're a friggin' bed and breakfast now! Apparently just renting rooms and apartments wasn't entirely satisfying for her. You just have to eat at 2 am.

This afternoon Mark and I helped Dad board up the front of the house while the building Northeast wind threatened to snatch the plywood boards out of our arms and the snow piled into gigantic banks during the first high tide. Low tide is when you have a chance to batten the house. We always help Dad with this job. Every storm. I love storms. I love the feeling of needing to defend our home from the raging elements. I love adventure and I love being outside and feeling it is us against the world - the world of weather. But, I don't want it to get TOO bad. This storm? This storm seems a little different.

LIZZIE!

Dad's affectionate name for me.
He hollers to Mark as the plywood board I am holding twists in my arms. I think it's going to fly. The wind devours voices.

MARK!!! Help your sister!

Mark leaps off the second seawall where he is staring out at the chaos of whitewater across the street waiting for the next big wave, grabs the other end of the plywood and we wrassle it up against the last pane of exposed glass on our new porch.

Lisa! Mark! C'mon! Back inside!

Dad grabs his tools, and we head out back to the cellar and climb the stairs to our back door. The next high tide - that one will be the test. This storm is building.

MARRRRRKKKK!!!!!!!!!!

Mom sends Karen and me out to get Mark. The storm is really getting going now.

WHAAATTTTTTT??????!!!!!

Drooooppppppppp the door!!! Mom says get inside!!!!!!!

I HAVE TO SAVE THE CAR!

I envision him drowned and martyred against the griffin logo on the grill of our newish SAAB station wagon. Ohmygod, does every Greek male have to have a friggin' messiah complex?! My brother has lost his mind.

LEAVE the friggin' car!!!!!!

Mark is standing in three feet of seawater with his soaked navy watch cap hiked down below his eyebrows and shivering like mad while trying to force the garage door back down and onto its track as each new surge of water barrels down the driveway. He's trying to prevent the car from being immersed in seawater. The four-foot, five-foot? snow banks encircling the house make this a fool's errand. The entire marsh is a new sea. Eldridge and Mile Roads are cut off. We are surrounded by water; if we want to get out now, we swim.

Let's grab him, Karen!

We don't have to. A huge wave rolls down the driveway, now a newly dug canal, and sinks Mark to his chest. The garage door is toast.

The rabbits! Good thing we moved our rabbits, Peter and Zonka, out of their hutch and into their storm dwelling way up inside the daylight cellar this afternoon. Their hutch usually sits right next to the garage. I hope it's a good thing. Do rabbits swim?

Mark finally concedes and wades over to the back steps. I love my little brother, and we hang out a lot, but I want to smack him.

WHAT ARE YOU? Friggin' ELEVEN???!!!!!!

Oh, yeah, you are.

This afternoon seems like years ago. Now it's 2 am and we're stranded on Wells Beach in a worsening storm and it's still two hours until high tide. In the warm kitchen, we sit rigidly on the mustard-colored cushions of the rock maple couch next to the granny stove crushing our mugs of cocoa in vice grips and listen with dread to the howling wind as each new surge crashes and tests the front of the house. The wind through the wires makes an unnerving high-pitched sound. This storm is relentless.

Mom suggests Karen and I sing, definitely signaling drug use or recent cognitive decline.

SING???!!!!!!!

Yeah, Karen and I have sung in the car on long road trips since, like forever, but I'm not really into belting out CLEMENTINE or THESE ARE A FEW OF MY FAVORITE THINGS right now.

Really, Mom?!

CRACK! Earsplitting crash. SLAM! The sound of splintering wood and the house rocks. The entire porch roof - it's a long porch - buckles and slaps against the front of the house. The lights go out. The next wave slams the front door open and cruises down the hallway like it's normal and splashes icy water through the kitchen. Kind of puts the kibosh on a late-night singalong.

WHERE ARE ALL YOUR FRIENDS???!!!!! WHY AREN'T THEY CALLING US??!!!!!!!
A voice that cannot be mine is screaming insanely.

CALL THEM!!!!!!!!

She cannot call. The phones are down. We have no choice now. We have to ride out this storm.

If You Don't Know A Knot, Tie A Lot!

Friggin' boat!

Who tied it up?!

I am almooooooost there......

Dang it!

Reaching with my right hand, mid-Crawl stroke, I am desperately swimming to catch our "Beach Kids'" styrofoam sailboat that a rare mid-summer howling northwest wind has ripped off its piling in Fisherman's Cove and is being blown straight out to sea.

Somebody's dad's friend gifted the bunch of us summer kids the hull of this former sailboat and we have spent all summer practically living on it out in front of my house. It can hold at least six fifteen and sixteen year olds at a time. You can stand up on it and dive off and, importantly - should extra chores be required of me in the late afternoon - it is handy to be out to sea and unavailable. In short, it is IMPERATIVE that I retrieve it. Just minutes before this moment:

The boat!

Gem hops up on the seawall and points out to sea at Fisherman's Cove. Noooooooo!!!!!

Seeing our summer plaything being blown offshore, I jump off the huge granite rocks below the seawall into the brisk 54 degree August seawater and begin a mad swim after it.

Ugh.....ALMOST!

Another wild gust blows it just out of reach again. I swim frantically on. I glance back for a second, Gem and Cindy trailing behind me. Gulping seawater I think:

What the fuck, no!! Do not follow me!!! You suck at swimming! You are not ocean swimmers - no friggin' training!

They are sawing at the water with flailing arms flapping from side to side in a parody of actual swimming. I feel a sudden and profound gratitude for Ms. Pomeroy, my longtime swimming instructor on the Riverside of Ogunquit Beach and the years of her commanding my sister and I to " jump in and swim to the sandbar now" in the 45 degree water of a 7:30 am June morning in Maine. Precision, expertise and no wasted stroke were her mottos and demands.

Living and growing up on the ocean and spending summers all day on Ogunquit Beach, my parents insisted my sister, brother and I take and pass the Red Cross swimming course schedule straight through Lifesaving. My sister and I are very strong swimmers. But, my summer buds, these two clowns?

My white whale catches another big gust and disappears from sight. I swim blindly on. Pulling out of a stroke and gulping air; I glance around for a second.

Holy fucking shit!

I am halfway to the earth's curve. Well, to the shipping lanes. Meaning, I am a long way from the seawall and land. I have never swum this far out to sea. Turning and looking back toward the seawall, a gallon of seawater propelled by a fierce chop careens down my throat.

Cough! Gag!

Well, at least French mainland kids will be psyched when they discover our boat on a Brittany beach. I give up hope of ever diving off it again. I look toward land again.

Crap, it's a long way.

The seawall is nearly a mile away against a stiff choppy sea. The northwest wind is now my formidable enemy; it's trying to blow me out with it. Twenty minutes of slogging, and I am tired. And, cold. One good thing: Gem and Cindy have long turned back.

Red Cross training, man. Thank you, Jesus. Oh, and, Ms. Pomeroy. I stroke on.

Gulp. Gag. I'm kinda developing a taste for seawater now; must be an acquired one - I've swallowed gallons. Mindlessly, I crawl and kick.

What I didn't know and couldn't really see this far away, was that, while my little drama was playing out, my parents, the Wells Beach fire department and a throng of ogling onlookers had lined the seawall waiting to see if we would make it. To see if I would make it. Not sure what the fire department's plans were. Unless that new ladder truck is secretly amphibious.

My dad was a lifeguard on Ogunquit Beach for years; I can only imagine what was going through his mind.

Dad is known as "Harry the Seal". He loves the ocean, he loves to swim and he taught the three of us to do the same. His body surfing skills are unparalleled. Well, except perhaps by my sister and me who, with such surpassing training and long days at the beach doing nothing but riding waves with our sleek youthful bodies, learn to ride clean into shore and beach ourselves in the sand. People routinely ask how we do it and we are eager to share but, apparently, it is a singular skill, not for the random tourist or Sunday beachgoer. Few pick it up. We had the best teacher.

The good news about my parents having the wisdom to insist on good swimming training is that not only do I know how to swim well, but also how to rest when tired - the good old Elementary Backstroke - and to pace myself. I dig, dig, dig with the Crawl and then, resting backstroke and back to the Crawl the entire exhausting way back.

At this point, JAWS the movie is just a spark on a dendrite in Spielberg's grey matter, but more pedestrian, run of the mill sharks lurking nearby suddenly occur to me and I freak out for a second.

Focus, man. Swim!
When I finally drag myself up the rocks to the seawall, cheers erupt.

Ohmyfuckingword, how embarrassing!

Am I shaking from the cold? Or from the cold reality of a stupid, life threatening mistake?

Mom grabs me swiftly and, in a quintessential Mom move, enfolds me in a green, wool army blanket, then ushers me in a walk of shame across the street to warm clothes and tea. The throngs stare.

When dry and warm, I want to go hang out with my friends like always but Mom's having none of it. I guess I scarred her for life. Again.

You need to stay here and rest until tomorrow, Lisa.

OHMYGOD, Mom! Really??!! I'm fine now!!!

You can be outside. Stay in the backyard ONLY! No, your friends can't come by! You need to rest.

Yeah, I scared the living shit out of her. Sorry, Mom! That really wasn't the point! The POINT was the boat. Friends. Freedom. Fun. What a blast we had with that friggin' stupid long-gone boat. Moan.

Wrapped tightly in wool blankets, I stretch out in the sun on the pink plastic chaise lounge in our backyard. I eye the kitchen window; I know she can see me.

I won't leave, Mom, sheesh!
Shiver.
I kinda don't wanna.

My omnipresent transistor radio sits beside me. It mocks me. "Gimme a beat boys and free my soul, I wanna get lost in your rock and roll and drift away....."

Fuck you, Dobie Gray! Too soon!
The warm August sun lulls me to sleep.

Later that week in a rare silent stretch at the dinner table, Dad chirps up. Being wry is his strength.

Good job, kid.
I was watching you, Lizzie. You were doing all the right things. But I was ready.

My obsession with staring glumly at my plate so I don't have to talk is momentarily paused.

Whoa. He was scared.
Remember this.

Another World

We have to get out on the roof. NOW!

My best friend, Janie hisses in a whisper to me while jamming her desk chair under the knob of her bedroom door. It is a rare night in midwinter when Mom has actually allowed me to stay over at Janie's house on Route One, Wells, where she lives with her pretty mom and younger sister. I can hear a man's voice that sounds scary coming from the kitchen. There's something wrong with the voice; I can't place what it is. Then, Janie's mom, barely audible, responds calmly. I can't make out what she is saying. The sound of breaking glass. Calm and steady voice again. The wall between Janie's bedroom and the kitchen gets hit with a force that makes it shake.

Janie and I have been best friends since she moved to Maine in sixth grade; we are now in eighth. We have such a blast together; she is an actual rebel and we smoke cigarettes together, steal our parents' small caches of liquor and hang out endlessly in our Wells Beach haunts. We purposely get stuck on Starfish Rock, a much-cherished rite of passage for every beach kid, and Janie laughs hard as I stand atop Starfish while the incoming tide maroons us and scream:

This is the end! Goodbye, cruel world!

She wets her pants. With my sweater tied around her waist to hide the shameful stain, we laugh so hard as we wade back through the tide I think I will wet my pants.

About a year after we form the anti-drug organization, SMARTEENS, at our junior high, and Janie becomes President and, I, Vice President, we confess to each other that we cannot find any science-based reason not to try marijuana and so, while receiving accolades for leading an anti-drug organization at our school, we become potheads. Our guilt gets to us so we resign.

She has never told me anything about her father. I didn't even know she had one.

Come on! Hurry up!

We struggle to get the frozen window up as quietly as possible and slip out onto the icy porch roof. We scuffle to the left of the window and huddle together by the edge of the roof. My cotton calico pajamas feel thin against the cold. We sit, hunched up, arms around our knocking knees and strain to listen if the voice is getting closer. It is.

JANIE!!!!!!!

The voice a mix of rage and anguish. Something slams into her bedroom door.

She has never told me anything about this; I have never known this kind of human behavior and I watch Janie intently for cues of how to act. We barely breathe. Janie stares straight ahead at the street light across the street. She's shaking. I eye the window in my periphery. The crazy voice quiets after a time and Janie leads me back to the window and, shivering like mad, we slide back in and head silently to bed. We leave the chair under the door.

In the morning, when we stumble bleary-eyed into the tiny kitchen, Janie's petite mom sits at the table holding a lit cigarette. The long ash drops onto the table. There is glass everywhere; a lamp lies smashed on the floor. The contents of an ashtray dumped on the counter. She manages a small smile. Her bottom lip is swollen and her right eye has a hint of the deep purple it will become. No one says anything about the night before and I do not ask.

One day some time after this, Janie finally tells me her family's whole awful story. This is after her Dad shows up one last time. He has his way with her yet again. This time, it ends with a bullet in his back. Her mom has had enough. Sadly, it doesn't kill him. He ends up in jail, but the years and years of Janie and her mom and little sister fleeing him and his sexual and physical abuse as they moved from place to place across the country cannot be erased. The damage done to Janie cannot be undone. So much damage done.

I look at the world very differently now. I wonder all the time about what really goes on with people. All. The. Time.

Born To Be Wild

"Listen to them, the children of the night. What music they make!"

A cool breeze flutters through the summer screen and Karen stops reading and shrieks.

OhmyGOD!!!!!! What WAS that?!

She grabs my shoulders and pulls me under her quilt with her. We cower. Then we contemplate who will reluctantly emerge first and investigate the nothingness that was the wind.

OOUUUCCHHH!

Her nails are digging into the thin flesh on my inner wrist.

C'mon, it's okay! It was the wind! Keep reading.

We cautiously peek out. Glancing nervously over my shoulder at the door to our shared bedroom, I want to hear more of DRACULA right now.

Hell's bells!

Her ONLY swear.
It's OKAAAAYY. READ.

My sister has been reading aloud to me since like forever. It doesn't matter that I read voraciously on my own; this is how we close most evenings before sleep. She reads me an uplifting bedtime story sure to aid in a restful dreamless night such as THE HAUNTING OF HILL HOUSE by Shirley Jackson, Stoker's DRACULA or BEST GHOST STORIES OF ALL TIME. We scare the living crap out of each other, howl with terror and laugh until we can't breathe at our insane fear of words on a page and things that just COULD go bump in the night.

Karen has been a constant in my life since I was born. She does many things for me. My older sister who really is perfect in every way - brilliant student, beloved firstborn, singer, storyteller, surpassingly clever playmate - has long been doing another enormous thing for me.

What the FUUUUUCCCKKKK???!!!!!!!!!!! BAM!

I only yell this once the asbestos door between the upstairs and downstairs is slammed and Mom and the distant kitchen are closed off. I accent that move with another splintering crash of my bedroom door. The psychedelic green plastic orb decorating my window clatters to the floor.

I am furiously writing in my notebook I cowardly hide under my mattress. Mom is so FREAKIN RIDICULOUS!!!!!!!!! Why can't I go to Robin's house tomorrow night?! EVERYONE is going!!!!! Fuck her!!!!!! I'm not FUCKING TEN!!!!!!!!! The lettering is the size of kindergarteners' block letters. I HATE YOU!!!!!!!

Small knock on my door.

What?

Lise, it's me. Can I come in?

Whatever. Sure.

I can never say "no" to her.

Karen gently eases my door open with a look on her face of such tenderness and anguish - years spent mediating these two impossible souls in her life who cannot find common ground for their infinite stubbornness - that I collapse on my bed. My anger of moments ago turns to misery and shame and then, always, tears.

I just wanna go out and be with my friends! Why is she so strict?!

She just worries, Lise. She doesn't know Robin's mom.

Why does she need to friggin' know Robin's friggin' mom? I don't wanna slide the OUIJA planchette around with Robin's MOM; I want to call on the spirits with my friggin' FRIENDS! Robin's flipping MOM has nothing to do with it!!!!! It's hard to swear properly in front of my sister; she's so good and doesn't really swear. Well, except for that one.

Lise, calm down. It's okay. Maybe you can invite Robin here?

I DON'T WANT ROBIN HEEEERRRRRE!!!!!!!!!! I want to go to HER house! Yes, I know, Lise. I want you to be with your friends, too. But Mom wants to be sure you're safe. Maybe she knows something you don't about Robin's mom.

AAARRRGGGGHHH. I HATE the "knowsomethingyoudon't" card! STOOOPPP!!!!!!!! Who cares what Robin's freakin' mom is like; she's about a hundred and eighty years old and will probably watch the Ten Thousand Dollar Pyramid all night while plucking her weirdly shaped eyebrows and scarfing Werther's caramels! Then we can safely play Truth or Dare and crank Tommy James and The Shondells' CRIMSON AND CLOVER all night to our heart's delight. We're not planning to shoot up. Not tonight anyway. What is wrong with everyone?!

Lise. Breathe. You're too worked up. You're making me worry. Just breathe.

Stop being nice! I am breathing; I'm breathing fucking fire! This longtime lockdown ain't working; I cannot WAIT 'til I decide who's nuts and who isn't on my own!

Collapsing in tears.

I'm not mad at you, Karen. Sorry.

Poor Karen. Why does she tolerate me? What a bad sister I am. She's just trying to help. What a wretched task. Maybe I'll stop being such a jerk when I realize I could lose her.

A Hard Day's Night

After you've scraped your cheek, place the Q-tip on the slide and gently roll back and forth. Clasp the slide by the edges and drop the second slide.....

Lisa. C'mon.

Dad's suddenly next to me at my lab table. What in the hell? Why isn't Dad teaching Chem class? It's 10:30. Why is he pulling me out of Biology with Coburn?! Not that I mind...
Nods between both teachers and we are out in the hall.

Your sister is sick; we're heading to Hartford.

Whaddaya mean? Why is Karen in Hartford? Where's Mom?

She left already. Let's go pick up Mark.

What?!

Karen was on a touring trip with the Bates College Chorale when she became violently ill in Sturbridge, Mass. An ambulance took her to Southbridge hospital but things kept going south and she was rushed to Hartford Medical.

Dad doesn't say much on the three-hour drive. I'm riding shotgun and Mark is practically on top of the armrest divider in our blue 69 SAAB bug. Seatbelts don't exist. Dad always lets me control radio stations. Paul McCartney croons through JET right now. It will become the anthem of this long and harrowing time.

In West Hartford, Dad leaves us at Uncle Tony and Aunt Billie's house with beloved cousins Susie, Linda and Amy and the three adults take off to join Mom at the hospital. We spend the first twenty-four hours of Karen's mysterious illness mostly entertained; we are young people skilled at games and creativity.

That night, Aunt Billie and Uncle Tony come home but not Mom and Dad. We're getting pieces of information here and there from Dad on the phone and from our aunt.

Dad: Lizzie, she is very sick. The doctors ask multiple times if she has recently been overseas, and what she's eaten. Low white blood cell count rules out appendicitis. They're looking at Dengue, Typhoid and Cholera.

She HASN'T been overseas and she's been vomiting for 24 hours and THESE are their questions?! Wow! Have they looked at Plague? Maybe it's Dropsy! Jesus Christ! This is a TEACHING hospital?! Clearly they've got a lot to learn - maybe they should try Med School! HOW many attendings does it take to diagnose a critically ill 19 year old??!!! (in this case those unable to number exactly NINE) Are you all suffering from River Blindness??!!! Friggin' DO something already!!!

Thirty-six hours have passed. My sister's temperature is hovering above 105 degrees Fahrenheit; she is completely delirious. I overhear Aunt Billie telling Uncle Tony that Karen thinks she is in a Nazi concentration camp and that Dad is with the SS. She keeps telling Mom they need to escape through the tunnel under her bed.

All four parents are at the hospital and we are now on our own on Westminster Drive. Sue, Linda and I take it upon ourselves to try to keep Amy and Mark, the youngest of us, entertained and distracted. Maybe we're trying to distract ourselves.

Let's go out back and play Continuation.

Sue, with a good idea; this is a favorite of ours. Whoever is "It" tosses up the soccer sized plastic ball and everyone runs, when the ball is caught that person is "It" and everyone has to freeze where they are. Then "It" tries to whack someone with the ball and they are out. Basically, it's freeform Dodgeball with a ton of hilarity.

It's late in the afternoon and no word from the hospital for a while. We are well into a rousing game when the always nimble Linda leaps up to avoid a hit and twists backwards landing into the split rail fence between the neighbor's house and theirs. When she hits the ground her leg is at an odd angle.

OOWWWWWW.

Linda's being stoic but she can't stand up. Susie runs next door to get Mr. Duluth; we need to get her to the hospital.

Oh, brother. Wait 'til our parents get a load of this. Wait 'til the hospital gets a load of this. We find out later they are deeply confused. Lotta confusion at this friggin' hospital. They might want to take a closer look at those wall certificates.

ANOTHER young girl with the last name Stathoplos in the ER? What?! Talk about freaking our parents out some more. We were actually trying to help, not make everything worse.

Now Sue and I are alone with Amy and Mark. Something is really wrong. No one is home yet; it's after ten. Aunt Billie had called around 6 PM to confirm Linda's knee was badly dislocated and they were keeping her overnight but they'd be back soon. They finally get back at 10:30.

How's Karen?

What is going on?!

Why aren't Mom and Dad coming back again tonight?

We have a million questions.

After Mark and Amy head up to sleep, Aunt Billie levels with Sue and me: They are going to operate.

Operate? That's GOOD, right? That will make her better?? Right?
My voice is a bit shrill.

Well, we hope so, honey. She is so ill she may not survive the operation. The doctors say she has a 50/50 chance. But if they don't operate she will die. They will go in like it is a burst appendix but they don't really think that's it.
WAIT! WHAAATTT??!!!!!! DIE????

My head is spinning and I feel like throwing up.

It has now been over forty-eight hours since Karen first became so ill on her trip and the doctors have done nothing. Maybe this will work.

Lying in the twin bed in the sewing room at Aunt Billie's that night, I look at the blue-gray walls and then stare up at the spackled ceiling and make this deal:

God? Yeah, hi, it's me - the one who doesn't believe in you? How's it going? Look, hear me out, okay? Take me. Take ME - NOT her. She is good; I am not. The stupid fat tears are leaking furiously out of my face and soaking the starchy pillow.

PLEASE! I know I don't believe in you but I'm gonna try, okay? Just for now - okay? No! I meant, like, for always, okay, OKAY?????!!! I will try. PLEASE! Not my sister, just take me instead!

Silence. More tears. Maybe a Faustian deal is a better bet.

When my parents finally show up at 6 AM in the morning, I am sitting on the carpeted stairway above the black and white parquet floor of the front foyer with Sue, Mark and Amy. Their faces give them away:

ohmygodmysisterisdead.

This horror lasts only seconds but I know the feeling will last a lifetime.

Dad: She's okay. She made it. It was her appendix; it burst in Sturbridge.

That was over two days ago. Dad looks like death. Mom looks like her skin is inside out. They collapse upstairs for a couple of hours before heading back to the hospital. Linda comes home on crutches that afternoon.

I overheard later that my sister died on the operating table mid-operation. She must have a crazy ass will to live on this nightmarish planet because they brought her back.

Jesus. I mean, GOD. Thank you, God.

It will be three more days before Karen is out of the ICU and Mark and I are allowed a brief visit. Mom tried to prepare us, but.....

HOLY SHIT!!!!

Don't show this, don't show this. She doesn't even look like her - she looks like a friggin' alien. She is covered in tubes - tubes in her nose and mouth, tubes in both arms, two coming from both sides of her gauze-covered abdomen. Her abdomen that has been sliced clear across and left unstitched; Mom has to be trained on how to clean the draining peritoneum that was chock full of the festering bacteria that almost killed her. Machines and blinking lights everywhere. She can't talk but when I come over she opens her eyes and they smile a little.

Hi, Karen.

The lump in my throat is growing exponentially and when we get back to the car I stuff myself in a ball in the back seat holding my knees and fight the stubborn tears.

A week later, Dad, Mark and I head back to Maine and school. Mom will stay in West Hartford with Karen. For a month. We drive down every weekend to see them. Paul McCartney and Wings fly with us always.

A month later when she is finally released from the hospital in Hartford, it is around the time of Greek Easter. We celebrate - all twenty-six of my Greek family - in West Hartford. It's always a raucous time. Out back in the quadrangle of the junior high that borders Aunt Billie and Uncle Tony's, we have our annual "flag" football game with Dad, Uncle Tony and Uncle Jesse. We practically kill each other and laugh and scream while diving for the precious pigskin. Linda is still sidelined. Karen is mostly refereeing and cheering us on. Glancing over at her during a lull, I see her. She's thin and pale but laughing and grabbing the ball. I also see a ghost behind her - the ghost of her. I shudder and return to the game. Looking back again:

Hey, Karen!

I do a goofy handstand and deliberately fall awkwardly to the ground. She cracks up.

She will be okay.

Heartbreaker

Hey, fucking RETARD! Hey, Judkins, Judhead! Dumbass! Why can't you walk? Fuck's the matter with you, you retarded? You fucking retarded?

Hallway by Mrs. Agren's room at 2:15 and my two personal shitforbrains are at someone they really go after. Swift kick to Daryl's right leg. They don't let up.

Retard! I'm talkin' to you, you fucking stupid moron! Didjya miss the bus? Ha, ha! Ya fuckin' asshole. Ya missed your damn bus!

Another kick. And another. Daryl buckles forward with a loud groan. He limps slowly toward the stairs to the buses, his right leg making a scuffing sound on the gritty brown tiles as he drags it. My heart is breaking. I don't know how to fix this. I am a homely and introverted sophomore. But I have watched this shit go down for way too long.

The most beautiful girl on earth - okay, the SECOND most beautiful girl, her older sister is THE most beautiful - Catie Towne rounds the corner to the stairs wearing a brilliant yellow cable cardigan with this strangely sexy green, red and yellow plaid pleated miniskirt. Her straight hip length golden brown hair shines like strands of tiny shimmering diamonds. Her green eyes are on fire. She is so friggin' gorgeous. She does this thing:

Hey! Stop that! Leave him alone!

She hollers this in the casual yet authoritative way that beautiful people always pull off because....well, because they are friggin' beautiful. She commands attention and respect. I desperately want to be her.

I have watched her sister, Maggie, on Ogunquit Beach in her groovy white bikini with the green ruffled top, hanging out at the lifeguard stand with all her hip friends since, like, time began. Being her seems so much better than being awkward, gangly me. She is the reason I wear a single strand of rawhide around my left ankle; she wears one and so that is what I take from her to make my own. She is beyond cool.

Catie stands stock still in the hallway, her look of simple outrage and deep concern is enough to thwart the thugs and send them skulking off. For now. The whole thing lasts about thirty seconds but it makes an indelible impression on me.

Next day on the bus ride home:

Hey, Daryl.

He picks his head up sleepily surprised.

Hey, Lisa, hi!

His words come out slowly, haltingly - like it's a struggle.

I sit in the seat in front of him.
Hi. How ya doin'?

We talk a little. As he shuffles to the bus door at his stop on Ledge Road, he turns and looks back at me, gives a rare smile. I'll sit next to him tomorrow.

Dancing With Mr. D

I start sneaking out to nightclubs to go dancing and drink with my two best buds, Terri and Jen. I am a junior in high school. Both are cool seniors; we play on the Varsity basketball team together and, in Terri's blue Volkswagen Beetle, we get up to all kinds of fun and mischief. My closest crowd now actually is the senior class more than my own class; they even choose me as the first female Class Marshall in the history of Wells High. Major shit. But, I do think it's pretty neat.

Saturday nights, though. Those are really fun. In Perkins Cove, there's a restaurant called The Old Cove House that turns into a disco dance club called The Nightdancer at around nine o'clock. This kid in my class, Scott Moulton and his parents own and run it. He's kind of new to Wells and really cool. He's got a moptop and wears a blazer but doesn't manage to look preppy or, worse, stupid - just looks a lot hipper than any of the other hippies and jocks and nerds in my class. We become regular customers at Scott's place. I accomplish this because I am an accomplished liar at this point, usually telling my unsuspecting parents that we are heading out to the movies in Portsmouth. It is amazing how many movies I've seen that I have never seen.

I order a Southern Comfort Sour because everyone else does; it's the drink of the moment. I am only seventeen but I look older, I guess. The drinking age is eighteen. I never really finish any drink because I just dance. I've never taken dance but I discover that my body just knows how to move to music and, even though I learn the Hustle and the Bump, I really just go with my own wild style. Apparently it is notable because I keep getting random people telling me I am

99

a great dancer. I gotta admit, it's pretty cool. We all dance like crazy every Saturday and it is my favorite thing. KC and the SUNSHINE BAND: "Do a little dance, make a little love, get down tonight....."

My parents don't seem to suspect anything out of whack until the night in January that Terri tries to kill me by deliberately whamming her car into a phone pole at the Moody light while driving me home. She's pissed that her boyfriend, who I wish was mine, is dancing next to me all night so, when dancing is done and Jen and Jackie and I pile into the Bug to go home in a snowstorm, she starts driving like a friggin' maniac and I plead with her to just let Jen and Jackie out of the car since it's only me she wants to kill. Nope. At the Moody stoplight, which Terri takes at probably 35 miles an hour, we go into a skid on the hard right turn and hit the phone pole. She maneuvers the VW out of the snowbank cushioning impact and gets us to the seawall in front of my house. I get out. Then she gets out, gives Jen the keys while staring at me with a big shiteating grin.

How was the movie?

Mom, spying me in the hallway.

Great, um, good. Yeah.

What the hell movie did I say I was gonna see? Shit. She eyes me suspiciously. Quick exit upstairs to bed. She might be on to me.....

I think it's probably the beginning of the end of Terri and me being friends but dancing has just barely gotten started. I wish I dared to take dance class; the idea of formal lessons is just plain terrifying. Herb Alpert and the Tijuana Brass tease me into it from years of listening to The Lonely Bull. My parents' eclectic taste - the Big Bands, Rachmaninoff, Sinatra, The Beatles - ringing through our house on Sunday afternoons. I want to languidly sway and sashay. So, as a freshman at Orono, I sign up for the legendary Teresa Gortowsky's Flamenco class; I even get the stupid castanets. I have no dance clothes. I wear a running outfit - an Adidas jacket with loose-fitting black pants. I feel like a fool. I am back to not eating very well and not liking my body, but I no longer starve myself for three days straight, binge eat 'til it hurts and then purge by abusing Ex-Lax like I did all summer. So. Progress.

I find her studio in Hamilton Hall, one of the campus buildings I've never even set foot in before, and my blood freezes; it is completely jam packed. Worse, jam packed with people who look like they belong in a dance studio. I look like I just got kicked out of the crab soccer game at gym class.

Mistake, mistake, mistake. Over and over in my head as I try to hide behind some handily tall male students who seem to follow her every step with ease. I can barely remember the first two steps in a sequence.

Ohmygod, ohmygod, get me outta here!

I drop Flamenco pretty quickly. It'll be three years before I enroll in another formal dance class.

It's Saturday night at York Hall, Orono, and keg party time on Third Floor. I don't want any beer. I don't wanna talk to anyone. Just spin the damn records - I came to dance. I wear the same patchwork mid length jean skirt Mom made for me in high school and a floral print shirt that passes my prerequisites and I dance alone all night. Wildly, with complete abandon. I've got the music in me. Me and Kiki Dee. I go to these keg parties a lot and it is always the same. I never stop dancing, I am soaked in sweat and completely in my own world. Right now it's ROCK AND ROLL by Zep - favorite song ever and my personal anthem. My hair whips around, my shapely legs and long arms are flying and the beat and me are one. Typically some random unshaven guy in a flannel shirt and three beers in, feels brave for half a second and weaves over.

Hey, wanna dance?

What the fuck do you think I'm doing? Idiot. Steven Tyler smokily suggests we WALK THIS WAY and Joe Perry with Aerosmith riffs on his guitar but I dance through the first verse only. I always enjoy walking out just before the last song. Keep 'em guessing.

Keep on moving. Moving is calming. Now, I think I'll start running. Running feels like prayer. Whatever that is.

When are you gonna do your first 5K?

Wanna run together?

I get this a lot. I'd rather swallow ground glass. I'm not interested in competition. I don't want pressure. I don't want to strain to keep up with you or slow down to accommodate your sluggishness. I just want to be alone and run. I don't wear a Walkman, I don't need music, I hate gyms and I don't wish for a treadmill. I just run. Outside. Every day. Only the wind, the trees, the road and my breath. Your 5Ks can take a hike.

School's Out

Ohmygod, can we PLEASE just get off Storrow Drive?!
We are sitting in traffic behind Boston Children's Hospital and I am reminded of glaciers. The turnoff for Route One North is light years away. Eternity will arrive sooner.

All I can think of is my Italian sub: Genoa salami, provolone cheese, juicy, ripe tomatoes, sweet, crisp Bermuda onions and lettuce drenched in oregano-laced Italian dressing. My mouth is watering. The iconic Sub Villa is still miles away on Route One, Saugus. Stopping at this sub shop on our way home is my favorite part of Mom, Dad and my routine trips from Wells, Maine to Boston for the past eight years. Pretty sure it's Dad's favorite part, too.

Just an hour ago, Dr. Zagreb opened my latest sheaf of X-rays and slapped each one onto his magic screen and, trusty calipers in hand, measured my now much-reduced curves.

Lisa, my dear. You are a success story for the books!

What?! You mean, I'm done?!

RARE EARTH in my head: "I just want to celebrate another day of livin'. I just want to celebrate another day of LIFE!!!!!!!!"

A maintenance program only, Lisa. Well done.

Holy shit. My serpentine spine is not straight - no spine actually is - but it no longer shoves all my internal organs into a throbbing ball. Mission accomplished! Why are my eyes filling up?

Years of physical therapy DONE. I don't know what I feel, really. I guess I'm glad but I like Dr. Zagreb; he's practically family now. The skeletal model in the corner is still smiling its death grin with stupid promise.

Fuckin A! I love you, man! I resist an urge to hug it.

I am relieved; it's been years of hard work and the pain is mostly gone. If it creeps in, I have the tools to push it back. I'm twenty-one. Only took eight years.

Spirit In The Sky

The Fan Club is packed tonight. This great spot owned back in the day by actress and commercial star, Julia Meade - one of Ogunquit's many claims to fame - is designed like a Japanese pagoda and perched high above and overlooking Perkins Cove. It was originally the Dan-Sing Fan. It's a cool nightspot for the late-night playgoing crowd from the Ogunquit Playhouse or just for people watchers and gatherers like me and my pals. Sometimes there's live music but no real dance floor. We dance anyway.

Tonight I'm hanging out on the balcony with some of the crew from my tour boat job while a sultry summer breeze wafts luxuriously through our hair when I decide to order a drink. I slip onto a barstool in the Japanese lantern festooned lounge and wait for the crazy busy bartender so I can order a Tom Collins. I don't really drink much but businesses usually don't open in order for you to just hang out so...yeah. Bee Gees tunes looping, "......night fever, night fever......"

Hi.

Soft and gentle male voice on my right. I turn toward it and have a rush of recognition - or something. As I order, the blue-eyed California surfer type sitting on the stool next to me smiles a radiant smile. I feel an instant connection. He is stunning to look at but, no, that's not it.

This is a crazy scene here, huh?
Yeah, I guess. You've never been here?

My long and blonde-streaked brown hair is hanging like a curtain across my face. My face that suddenly feels flushed. His eyes and his spirit - definitely his spirit - pull me in. John Fogerty and Creedence are wailing out their version of "I PUT A SPELL ON YOU" in my head. What in HELL is going on?

No, no. I've never been here. I'm just traveling around.

"Traveling around" - wow! At nineteen and stuck in college, this epitomizes my ideal life. We talk of the meaninglessness of everyday life. Astral planes come up. We talk about the universe and past lives and, holy crap, this connection is profound. We sit staring into each other's eyes and gobbling up each other's thoughts and words like divine food for our souls. The noise and crowd of The Fan Club disappear; we are alone in a galaxy of our own.

Do you know about Eckankar?

Shit. New rock band? I'm rolling through WBLM's catalogue in my mind. I have no idea who or what Eckankar is and don't want him to know it but he sees and it's okay.

Eckankar, he says, is this whole spiritual journey thing as a way to experience God and our souls. Astral plane travel is a groovy piece of it.

I'm ready to sing "Hu" to my heart's delight if it means I can hang out forever with this wildly familiar soul I am looking at. We leave the bar. We're going to the beach; it's like eleven o' clock at night but I feel strangely safe and calm with Jeff. His name is Jeff. In the parking lot, I comfortably get into his car - a beige VW bug with an old metal roof rack and, of course, the unmistakable blue and yellow license plate of California. I eye him once more. He doesn't look anything like Ted Bundy.

At the beach we walk for hours and never stop talking. There is no physical requirement and sex seems entirely irrelevant while being with this fellow traveler in the universe. He does kiss me goodnight at my door, which is lovely. Really lovely. We spend two nights doing this same thing: walking the beach holding hands, feeling connected on some strange and new spiritual level - something I have never felt with any other human before this - and discussing everything spirit and otherworldly. He teaches me about Eckankar.

And, then, as fast as he appeared, he is gone. So weird. I don't feel a hole in my soul. When I get back to Orono, I find a group practicing Eckankar and join immediately. Jeff's spirit stays with me.

You Wreck Me, Baby

FUCKFUCKFUCKFUCKFUCK!!!!!!! WHY is this bill coming to me HERE??! To my friggin' HOUSE where MY PARENTS live??!!!!! Are you fucking KIDDING ME??!!!!! Friggin' mailman, REALLY????!!!!!!! Why do I have to have such a stupidly ridiculously recognizable last name??!!!!! The bill says: Lisa Stathoplos 346 York Hall, Orono, Maine! Fucking O-R-O-N-O!!!!!!! As in: PERENNIAL CROSSWORD CLUE! As in: NOT FUCKING WELLS BEACH, MAINE!!!!!!!!! THIS is Fisherman's Cove Inn, 257 Webhannet Drive - super fucking different than ORONO because of the fucking SPELLING!!!!!!! What the fuck is wrong with you??!!!!!

I race upstairs, past the asbestos door and down the hall to my old room. EPIC SLAM!!!!! Walls shudder. Hot tears exploding out of my eyes. How am I ever going to explain to her WHY I am getting a bill from a Sanford hospital we would NEVER go to??!!!!!!!

FUUUUCCCKKKK!!!!!

Small knock.

Lisa? Can I come in?

Oh, Jesus Christ, here we go.....Mom comes in; her eyes are all puffy and red. OHMYGOD! I have spent my life keeping hard things from my mom because she seems so naive about their reality in my life and she gets all sad and serious and I can't stand it. Then, it becomes all about HER - about me taking care of HER needs. What about ME?! I'M the one going through this!

Mike Nolton left me pregnant and took off across country to chase his stupid dream of owning a Toyota Land Cruiser and being a California surfer poet. Kill me now! Land Cruisers are for surfer wannabes and your poetry makes Rod McKuen seem esoteric! My entire junior year at Orono I got up at 5 am and slopped greasy day-old ham steaks and slimy poached eggs that brought up bile just seeing them out of the corner of my eye to the four dorm Quad at York Commons in order to pay for the abortion our tawdry union necessitated. Now, because the oblivious mailman is COMPLETELY INCOMPETENT I'm gonna have to fess up to Mom what I spent a year successfully hiding!

Soft and quiet voice.

Why couldn't you tell me? So I could help?

She's distraught. Ugh! I can't handle distraught - anger is preferred.
Tears stream down her former model's face.

Mom! Stop! How could I tell you this if when you caught me smoking it was the end of the known world? We made our bed together, you and me, Mom!

And, it says here, July 15th - my birthday.
More tears.

OHMYGOD! YES!!!!! It was horrible! I had the procedure, he left me that night with a Dear Jane poem - I think it was an indecipherable Haiku - and then I rode my Schwinn from my room above Maxwell's Store in Ogunquit to

Webhannet Drive in order to see you on your birthday while cramping and gushing buckets of blood into an inadequate pad! I NEVER wanted you to know. I even made a pact with a god I don't believe in to never do it again so I wouldn't writhe in hell for all time but, I'm having one of my feelings that I'll screw that up, too, and I think I'm getting a faint whiff of brimstone....

Of course, I can't tell her how he returned a month ago, took little old broken-hearted me for a ride on his stupid Triumph Bonneville 500, forced me to have sex with him while having my period with me pushing him away and pleading with him:
Please, no, I have a tampon in!

I tried fighting him off while he pinned my thin arms over my head in his jacked construction worker way. I couldn't find that stupid tampon for two weeks - that's how jammed up inside me it was. Upper body strength really takes a hit in the female body. THEN! Guess what, Mom? He left again for good. Yeah, I'll keep that shit to myself.

And no way would I tell her about that other time in high school when someone I thought was a friend got me drunk at a party and took advantage of me while I was passed out on his mother's bed. That time I woke up bewildered in the middle of him slamming into me which hurt like hell. He drove me home later that night in his forest green Mustang and we never spoke of it again.

I'm sorry, Mom. I'm okay now.
Hug.

It's okay.
I hug her again.

My penance: Take care of everyone I love who cannot handle my truth. Deal with my truth later. Sigh. Mom picks up the box of Kleenex and wipes tears on her way out. I wonder if she's gonna tell Dad.

It took my college roommate to tell me that the word for these events is "rape". But the thing is, I only know maybe two women who do not share an experience like this. It's the seventies and we are taught by our culture that any rape is our own fault. Susan Brownmiller recently published AGAINST OUR WILL, so this rape culture of victim responsibility and no male accountability is gonna change real soon.

Ha, right. That was the NINETEEN SEVENTIES.

True Love

Do you need a ride home?

Oh, hi, Todd, okay, thanks!

Our relationship starts as friends and boat cohorts. I worked for Todd's parents on their tour boats and, when he ended up going to UMaine/Orono, we started hanging out. Actually, he befriended me following my disastrous relationship and heinous breakup that left me devastated for a year. He's insanely shy but when we are together his quiet insistence makes anything seem possible. The idea of romance never crosses my mind; he's younger than me and not tall enough. I need tall. Paul Bunyan might do.

We go up to his freshman orientation at Orono in late June and immediately blow off the incoming students' agenda and start scouting bodies of water in the area. I've been here for two years but it takes Todd to make new and exciting things possible. We discover how close we are to the ocean of the midcoast; we cruise to Schoodic Point, Winter Harbor, Belfast and Rockland. The idea of weekends spent camping comes up. I've never really camped - I'm an ocean girl but everything with Todd sounds like fun. A whole new world is opening up to me.

We rent a crappy fiberglass canoe that won't point up for shit and throw it into the Stillwater for a spin. The northwest wind is howling. Okay. Lesson learned. Paddle upwind first! Ride the breeze home when you are tired. Got it. After grinding our way back in the canoe which is completely incapable of making good forward way, we are exhausted and educated. We portage the stupid metal crap canoe back to the car. Todd knows he should have known better and is shaking his head. We crack up. It was fun.

Lise, you hungry?

Oh, no. The food thing. Do NOT act weird.

Yeah, sure.

In Rockland, we stop at this big diner, ALL DAY BREAKFAST plastered in giant lettering on its towering sign. It looks like it's been here for a hundred years - that sagging roof could stand an update. Todd orders the Fisherman's Breakfast: a cheese omelet the size of a frying pan, home fries with ketchup and homemade english muffins smothered in butter. I am absolutely starving. Well, when in Rome... Matching heaping plates appear. I stare down at mine feeling trapped. My plan is to eat as little as possible. I devour the entire thing. What the hell?! Traveling with Todd means we eat together; it makes it a lot harder to pretend to eat. I am actually really hungry. We are always on the go; appetites build. Is this what normal is?

Next time we go up to Orono it's to check out his digs at Hancock Hall. Later, driving around the midcoast, we come upon Toddy Pond - yes, really! Toddy Pond! We spot an old wooden Kennebec canoe with its canvas torn to shreds, broken ribs and both stems complete goners. But the LINES! Todd tells me the sheer is absolutely beautiful.

Can you see it, Lise?!

No, but I'm starting to. I am learning all things nautical; "sheer" is important. The canoe has a "FREE" sign on it. Well, that's handy. Todd can't believe what a beauty it is so we grab the sad old thing and decide to fix it.

This becomes our after-work project of the summer. In the basement of his parents' three-story summer rental, the Hutchins House, we scrape and remove blackened varnish, pull out the destroyed seats, take them to be recaned. Todd teaches me about "sister" ribs, brightwork and thwarts.

The two stems, though, are going to be tough. Long strips of white ash need to be laminated and then, ever so gingerly steamed and bent around the hull to give that classic shape to a double-ender wooden canoe. Todd, coming from his remarkably self-sufficient wooden boat family knows how to do all of these things. His handcrafted wooden skiffs are legendary. Especially the ones the mean and jealous Kurt Fowler has cut loose to be lost at sea. Special guy, that Kurt. He could be the original inspiration for anger management.

Every single evening after long, sometimes ten hour days, working for Todd's parents on their boats - he as captain and me as tour guide - we retire to the dirt floor basement of the Hutchins House and toil late into the night on what is definitely becoming a more daunting project than we had anticipated. But, we remain happy and optimistic; we will have a refurbished, beautiful wooden canoe to take back with us to Orono a month from now.

Each night when we pack it in, Todd gives me a ride home on his classic Bultaco dirt bike. It is always chilly in August and he gives me his beat-up navy blue down coat to wear and I cling cozily to his thin frame with my face buried into the nape of his neck - no helmets - for the whole seven-mile ride home. This is my favorite part of the night. I never want the ride to end.

Wait a minute. Don't screw up this friendship. No kidding, okay! The voice in my head is getting irritating. But, what is this feeling I'm feeling?

One night Todd is working on the bow stem. Again. This is the THIRD bow stem; the other two snapped during the delicate process of bending the white ash. Todd managed those two incidents with amazing grace. A lot of work is required before the bending procedure and infinite patience and caution are a big help. But! We are getting close to the major step of recanvassing; it's starting to actually look like a canoe. We're practically paddling midstream already! Steam is roasting Todd's face as he carefully urges the reluctant ash to curve just a few millimeters more. SNAP! The stem breaks.

MOTHERFUCKER!!!

Tools start flying. A hammer whizzes by me and makes a clanking sound as it hits the water heater. C-clamps are hurled to the ground with a vehemence that leaves multiple imprints in the dirt floor and empty varnish buckets are kicked into oblivion past the oil tank. But it's what comes out of Todd's mouth that sticks with me. I thought I was well-versed in colorful language but swears to make the gang at the bait wharf blush are gushing from Todd in an endless litany of body parts I've never even heard of doing things to your mother or distant relatives with a violence I never knew possible. None of this is directed at me but it is so out of character for this gentle soul who I've been acquainted with for years ever since he sat behind me in band playing third clarinet in eighth grade, that I cower by the cellar door waiting for the storm to pass. I'm thinking it's about more than a broken stem.

When we finally finish the canoe in late August, it is a marvel to behold with the gleaming red canvas and near-perfect brightwork as well as the stunning lines. When we hoist it atop Todd's red compact Subaru - instantly christened "The Canoebaru"- people stop to ask us about it and marvel at its beauty everywhere we go.

Back in Orono, when we launch in the Stillwater and slice our paddles through the cool fall water it is a dream come true. Todd in the stern steering, and me up forward in the bow, it points up into the wind like magic and moves through the water with unheard of stealth and ease. James Fenimore Cooper's gotta be looking down at us - a modern day Hawkeye and Chingachgook - doing he and those last Mohicans proud.

I get pregnant again. With Todd. It's unfair because we screwed up ONCE. That is THE TRUTH! Yeah, we always messed around but stopped short of intercourse because "fool me once" and like The Who promises: WON'T GET FOOLED AGAIN! We are gonna have the baby; we have it all decided. But, our parents - all four of them - intervene; they say our lives will be ruined. I succumb to the pressure and never really know whose decision I am making - seems like it's everyone's but mine. And it's my body. My reality, not theirs. So, if the Catholics turn out to be right, I'll skid down to my doom in as epic an exit as all my theatrical training can manage while serenaded from above by BOTH Jimi AND Stevie Ray shredding VOODOO CHILD on their pearly white Stratocasters.

Let's Dance

I'm trying Beginning Ballet at The Thomas School of Dance in Bangor, Maine. I still suck at pickup but tenacity kicks in and I persist. I am going to get dance training if the embarrassment kills me. The studio is just down the road from Todd's and my apartment, which is right down the road from Stephen King's house. Could be ominous.

Oh, yeah: Todd and I fell madly in love, got pregnant, had an abortion to please our parents and then got married to spite them - me at 22 and Todd at twenty. So, I'm married now even though I've never believed in marriage. I mean, I believe it EXISTS. Another sacrament bites the dust and the Eternal Hippie Garden Gate just creaked a little bit closer to shut.

Once I earned my Theatre Arts degree I could not wait to get out of Orono and move back south to my home in Ogunquit. But, Todd got mononucleosis in the fall of his sophomore year and had to take the year off to recuperate. I was a senior. He had three years to go before he could earn his degree. When I graduated and we got married, I did get out of Orono and move south - all the way south to Bangor, seven miles away. Sigh. So, three more years in the greater Bangor area for me. That was never my plan. Todd does finally earn his Mechanical Engineering degree. The truck is packed with our meager belongings and our two cats, Sassafrass and Rodie, and we trundle down Broadway. I wink at Stephen King's wrought iron bat fence surrounding his striking red Victorian style house for one last time as we leave Bangor for good. At last we are moving home.

Thomas School of Dance made me brave. I pliéd and relevéd through an entire session of ballet class without walking out in abject shame. I decide to take a class in Portland at Casco Bay Movers Dance, a jazz company. I've been driving three or four times a week and to my Beginning Jazz classes with Katlyn Blackstone and Sheila Bellefleur for about two years. Yeah, two years of Beginning Jazz. I have at long last nailed a pas de bourrée and can get across the floor with chaînés turns, no longer dying of mortification before hitting the halfway point. Snickering has ceased. Okay, no one snickered but they should've. I can even track a simple combination. I am actually finally comfortable in a dance class; yeah, it's a Beginning Class but you shoulda been around for the first two years. What a fuckin' nightmare! Every. Single. Class. Invariably, I arrive home in Ogunquit after a 40-minute drive, my face slathered in snotty tears, my wracking sobs squelched by my Peugeot 504's radio blaring Talking Heads BURNING DOWN THE HOUSE or Phil Collins' I DON'T CARE ANY MORE or whatever is on WBLM. I nearly drown in self-pity. I swear I will not go back. But, fuckin' A, I do.

Sheila pulls me aside after dance class one day. She is very petite and adorable with huge wide set eyes in a lovely heart shaped face and she is an amazing dancer; I have watched her and her Movers perform for years. Apparently, she has watched me onstage. I am a professional actor now. Yeah. That happened. I get paid to work onstage.

Lisa, I think you might want to move on to Intermediate dance classes.

Wow. She may as well suggest I pair skate with Peggy Fleming.

Really?

I am both thrilled she has noticed and scared to make that leap. But I do it. Next class with Lily, well-known technical perfectionist in the Movers and who seems quite full of herself. But, holy crap! I am dancing next to the brilliant Larry Lee Van Horne who I have watched dance with Ram Island and Portland Ballet Studio as well as the Movers. Other accomplished dancers are in class as well. I am not screwing up. Well, at least not royally. I feel at home in a studio - something I never ever thought possible. I am not the best but, when I dance, I have my passion and my expression and it makes a simple pirouette feel righteous. I take jazz, ballet, modern, African - I cannot get enough. I will never be a professional dancer, but I am a pretty good amateur. I study with other companies; I dance in a repertory company, I choreograph for the theatre and for recitals. I become a member of an intergenerational modern dance company in Portland. Dance is the number one thing - the number ONE thing - that makes me a better actor because I am finally truly in my bones. My entire body, heart, mind and soul are now my instruments to bring a character to life. I got great training in a small theatre department at UMO - Stanislavsky, Meisner, Chekhov, Hagen, you name it - but dance gave me my body to feel comfortable in. I take classes always now. I end up taking routine dance classes for twenty-seven years. I stick with it. I guess I'm tenacious.

Are you a professional dancer?

I get this a lot.

No, no.

Secret smile. The passion I always had. The discipline to obtain technique and some mastery was hard won.

Trippin' The Life Fantastic

Lex Luther is strapped to the hood of Karl's forest green circa 1975 Volvo station wagon. It's pretty dark so his magenta shirt and green pants look colorless. He's still a rock star. It is 4 am and me and my fellow actors of Maine Theatre are heading up to Freeport - destinations L.L. Bean and The Desert of Maine. We are going because during our routine post-show Bacchanal this evening and while watching my first porn film, Debbie Does Dallas, I admit in some drunken conversation thread that I have never been to either of these places.

Tina: That's it! Let's go!

We pile into Karl and Dale's cars. There's about eight of us making the trip. Windows open, summer night air blowing our hair, we are singing "...some enchanted evening...." at the top of our lungs and laughing our heads off cruising up 295 to Bean's - famously open seven days a week, twenty four hours a day, three hundred and sixty five days a year. Lex is our mascot, and has been ever since someone found him stuck in Karl's couch on Grant Street. He's about the size of a standard Ken doll and, oh, the things he's been witness to. Thank God he can't talk. This company, this life is what I turn to after four years in the theatre program at UMaine/Orono. It feels perfectly perfect because it is.

When I graduate college; my seven fellow Theatre Arts graduates head to seek their fortunes wherever. Scott and Carleen and Frances and Gail all traipse off to The Big Apple to try their luck. I envy their courage but have no desire to go to a big city and even less desire to try my hand at real professional theatre yet; I'm just scared shitless. I get a couple of small roles at Acadia Repertory in Bangor but slink back into the shadows earning a stipend for running lights or stage-managing shows; I don't want to really put myself on the line as an actor yet. I can't even bring myself to call myself one. But, Katherine Nolan of Off-Broadway and Obie-winning fame, along with the talented Maine Theatre gang, won't let me hide; they've been watching me onstage at Orono for years and they drag me into a new life in the professional theatre. "They" are a group of classically trained New York Equity actors who, after years of performing at Acadia Rep, have fallen in love with Maine and have decided to stay and create a new company here. Katherine is, hands down, the most extraordinary actor I have ever seen on any stage and I hold her and her work in complete reverence. Never in my wildest dreams do I think she will become my mentor and fellow company member.

We pull into the parking lot of Bean's, which, remarkably, has a few cars in it. We fall out of the car, yell at Lex to "wait here - we'll be right back", double over in gales of laughter, and head in. Not much memorable about the store probably for either party - us or Bean's. I imagine they are fairly accustomed to troupes of traveling actors, giddy with drink and no sleep, giggling hysterically at ghoulish taxidermy or finding fly fishing equipment inanely hilarious and swiftly moving on. We tumble out of Bean's, salute our comfortably plastic Lex and clamber back into the car.

Following the camel signs we finally locate Desert Road and pull into the Desert of Maine. It looks vaguely wan and pathetic in the pale moonlight. A child's sandbox comes to mind. I don't know what I expected. I've climbed the pyramids of the sun and moon outside of Mexico City. I envisioned something at least akin to one of the back sand dunes at Ogunquit Beach. No such luck. I burst out laughing.

This is it?! Are you guys kidding? THIS is what all those friggin' camel billboards from York through Portland are heralding? We nearly die laughing.

Side note: I have since belonged to and worked for multiple professional theatre companies in my long career - none have been as professional AND as FUN as Maine Theatre.

Maine Theatre now has a home in the basement of Waynflete School in Portland's West End. But, we also tour; it's summer. Katherine and I are kickin' it in John Ford Noonan's A COUPLA WHITE CHICKS SITTING AROUND TALKING and Lagraffe and Duffy are smoking hot in Shephard's TRUE WEST. We bring down WHITE CHICKS in Orono one night and close Pat's Pizza hanging out with my former formidable theatre professor, Dr. James Bost, his theatre bud, Joe Foster and my favorite theatre professor, Al Cyrus, along with a ragtag crew of Orono theaterites.

Around 2 am we're driving towards Bangor in Lance's VW bug, and Katherine, sleepily and in her classic nasal drawl, announces something to me.

Oh, this couple whose house we're staying at tonight? Yeah, they have five Weimaraners.

What the fuck is a Weimaraner? I query.

Yawning and driving one-handed:

They're trained attack dogs, but, don't worry, I have the key to the side porch and they know we're coming.

My heart is somewhere around my knees and pumping like mad.

What the fuck, Katherine, are you SURE?!

She's infuriatingly nonchalant. We drive up. She fumbles for the key and unlocks the door and we tiptoe in. No sound. Phew. I sleep fitfully in the big brass bed next to Katherine in this nameless couple's house. Friends of the theatre, I guess.

The sun comes pouring in early the next morning and I awaken to Katherine's empty side of the bed. She is down the hall making a phone call, I guess. Suddenly, I hear the staccato click, click, click of dog claws on hardwood and, badabing! One, two, three, four and number five Weimaraner make a semi-circle neatly around the bed, sit on their haunches and stare at me. I pull up the thin sheet for reinforcement. Hoarsely:

Katherine?

A bit more forceful now:

Katherine?! There are five dogs in here!

She patters in, shoos them easily and we live to tell the tale. Jesus Christ.

Touring on another night, we close the show and head to an empty camp on a lake in Orrington that belongs to somebody's mother's cousin or something.

We are all particularly wild and crazy on this night, thrilled to have this sprawling summer place all to ourselves. The hashish and the drink flow freely as is our custom and a few things stand out in my substance-fueled blur. Me sitting on Katherine's lap as she strokes my face sensuously, confessing how she has always been so attracted to me. It is the first time I feel something akin to sexual toward another female and it is at once intoxicating and wonderful to think that my idol idolizes me.

Later in the crazed evening, Richard, Karl and Michael have procured some fresh eels from the lake that they plan to roast somehow. Like you do. Right now, we are all summoned into the bathroom to observe the tangle of slithering blackness swimming about in a giant mass in the homeowner's unsuspecting clawfoot tub. I stifle a rising shriek caught in the back of my throat but, like almost every other crazy Maine Theatre thing, a tubful of black eels seems almost entirely normal and peals of laughter the correct response. Sometimes when I look back on this moment I see Tina sitting IN the tub with the eels. This cannot be right, but there it is.

Somewhere in the wee hours, we all finally tumble into bed - the same bed for five of us for some reason - Dale, Tina, me, Michael and Katherine. It is truly insane. I have a wicked crush on our hunk of a director, Dale, so I don't mind all the legs and snoring and crushed arms. Just another night on the road.

In the bleary-eyed morning someone is cooking eggs - really? Ugh. I wander out to the dock where Lex is being photographed before his lap across the lake. An engine roars out of the blue and a motorboat nearly drowns Lex but Karl acts swiftly, jumps in and grabs all twelve plastic inches of him before he dithers down to lake bottom. Soaked but intact, we strap him back onto the hood of the Volvo. Time to head back to Portland. Another show tonight.

F. Parker Reidy's late night restaurant and bar on Upper Exchange, Portland, is the only place open late after shows. We are all hunkered in the back of the bar after bringing down Durang's BEYOND THERAPY and are scarfing small steaks and french fries. Heineken bottles and shot glasses are scattered all over the table. On the way to the Ladies Room I hear:

Why aren't you in New York or LA?

I get this a lot and I'm fairly certain by this point these people don 't mean Lewiston/Auburn. I have been pretty lucky - really lucky, I guess, since I made the decision to try my hand at professional theatre, give myself two years before I reassess and either continue on or call it quits. I cannot remember when two years were up. I hear this line often after shows come down and I try to sneak out of the theatre before I have to expose my vulnerable self to always anxiety-provoking post-show talk.

I work for Maine Theatre, Maine Acting Company, The Theatre at Monmouth, Durham CenterStage, Vintage Rep, Worcester Forum - always in major roles. When I show up, I get parts. I don't want to live in a major city but, okay, I will go and spend a week in New York and see what happens. I have an agent in Portland now, Laura Butterworth, who I use for commercial work and film, industrial videos, voiceover - hot in the eighties - which I do plenty of and make great money doing. She sets up a bunch of auditions and I head to the Rotten Core to stay with my beloved and benevolent Aunt Becky, Senior Editor for Sports Illustrated, on the Upper West Side.

It's not like I haven't come to New York to audition before. I came up here to audition for an ad for a national furniture company. I got it. So I had the opportunity to hawk the notion that the right dining set could mean everlasting joy. And, the first time I came to the city, I was sent by another Portland agent to attend this crazy talent competition thing where a crush of hundreds of model wannabes, accompanied by throngs of their insane wannabeevenmore mothers, strutted and twirled and danced their way to certain oblivion for Talent America. That time, I got an award: Most Promising New Actress. Even got a cheesy gold foiled statue made to look like an Oscar. Jesus Christ. Actors sell their souls at bargain basement prices.

Barbara Rosoff of the venerable Portland Stage, Equity house in Portland, knows my work and has expressed interest in casting me in their opening show this season. The catch is, I have to go to New York to audition for the casting director per Equity LORT house rules. So I go to a couple of other auditions as well. It's summer and hot and muggy and my very low city tolerance is close to reaching its breaking point when I head to the LORT house cattle call. It's attended by a bunch of casting directors and agents who will decide your theatrical fate. I have my prepared pieces - Lady Macbeth and Viola - what a friggin' naive idiot I am. Rule Number One of auditioning: never use well-known or classic pieces! Oh, well. I join the crush of actor wannabes in the hallway of some nondescript downtown building.

Oh, joy. "Wangy Actorini Talk". My term for the way actors put on this show of being connected in "the business" by dropping names, talking shop and/or next gigs or last gigs or upcoming auditions. I hate it. I am used to it, but I hate it. No one is actually connecting with each other; everyone is showing off in this false and grossly pretentious way. Gag. Get me outta here.

I go in. I do my thing. I now cannot wait to get out of the city and head back to blessed summer in Maine. Providence provides. Barabara Rosoff offers me the part of Chick the Stick in CRIMES OF THE HEART at Portland Stage. Yup. I had to come all the way to New York to be cast in a show the director already knew she wanted me for back in Maine. Welcome to regional theatre. Insanity. But, it's a friggin' sign! I am supposed to stay in Maine. Hooray! Bye, bye, NYC! I cannot wait to rush out of the building and the city. Random female Casting Director or Agent - I'm not sure which - stops me, leans across the table and slides her card at me while holding me firmly with what seems a meaningful gaze.

When you decide to come back to New York, call me. I want to sign you.

Rosoff nods at me knowingly. Wow. Just like that. I have pals who haven't been able to get an Agent after years here.

Okay. Yes, thank you, I will.

I know I am never coming back.

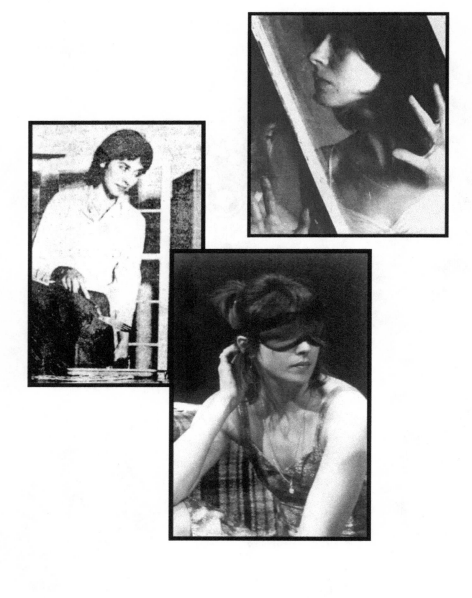

I Discover U-235

WOULD I LIE TO YOU?!

Annie Lennox and the Eurythmics howling into the night from my Philips transistor radio. Fuck. Shit. Damn. Cesium 137. Strontium 90. Radioactive isotopes. Fission. Uranium 235 - shit! What's the half-life of U235? I used to know this by heart. Oh yeah, 700 million years or something like that.

Ohmygodohmygodohmygodohmygod. I hate being right all the time.
C'mon! Bring Lennox back! This cannot be real.
Straining to hear the announcer on WTOS/Sugarloaf, I can barely breathe.
Announcers NEVER interrupt rock stations:

partial meltdown of reactor number...

what? where? .....huh? Chernobyl? Where the fuck is?.....

Radioactive gases released ....Sweden detecting radioactive particles.....

ohmyfuckingword!..... the station is going in and out.

It's around 4 am on April 25, 1986 and I am freezing and huddled under quilts in my icy room at Cumston Hall, The Theater at Monmouth, listening to music and delaying getting up for another long day of touring: three shows in southern Maine today. It' s Viola in TWELFTH NIGHT this time. Now, time is frozen.

Everything about nuclear power and water-cooled reactors that I have feared and protested against for years is playing out in a small town about a hundred miles north of Kiev, Ukraine. Images of worldwide nuclear winter and the end of the world cloud my brain.

My arguments to convince people nuclear power is not safe have never gone for the jugular - the core meltdown and legendary China Syndrome, which is the uncontrolled drilling down of radioactivity from one side of planet Earth to the other. No, I always use my power of persuasion to emphasize the difficulty in storing spent fuel rods safely for thousands of years. Like, 10,000 years to be precise. Whether in the Bangor Mall trying to convince random shoppers willing to suspend their consumerism for two minutes to listen to my exhortations of the pernicious threat nuclear power poses or tramping with my flyers while dodging barking dogs between houses on Stillwater Avenue for the Maine People's Alliance or picketing the Seabrook plant near Portsmouth, New Hampshire or the relatively new Maine Yankee in Wiscasset, I patiently make my case. I write my senators and representatives and send letters to the editors of local papers.

50ish white male outside Day's Jewelers in downtown Bangor:

My goodness, you really have your facts down!

Why is it so hard to believe a twenty something hippie girl knows her shit? Hey, Chuck! Or, whoever you are. I come from a friggin' family of scientists. My uncle DESIGNS reactors! Yeah, he works out of Hartford for Combustion Engineering and freakin' helped design Maine Yankee. Neat, huh? Complicated is an understatement; I love my uncle. He loves me and my spirit. You oughta be at Thanksgiving dinners when, in the midst of the cacophony of twenty-six people sharing amusing family anecdotes, we veer off topic to nuclear power - FUN! I had BETTER know my stuff going head-to-head with a nuclear engineer.

I swing my feet out from the cozy covers and they land on the cold floor. When I meet my fellow actors at the breakfast table no one seems aware yet. Maybe they are still recovering. I beat all their asses at poker last night and I think I cleaned up almost twenty bucks in change.

I've never played poker before.

Ha, ha! Yeah, sure, okay, we'll keep that in mind, Lisa.

Tim, while shuffling the sticky deck and lining up blackjack.

Big round of community chuckling.

We played well into the night. Pocketing my change later on I think how I can really use it for the pile of laundry building up in my room upstairs and smile. I really never had played poker before.

All of this seems eons ago now. The world feels upside down and, even with a gorgeous central Maine sunrise, it seems suddenly dark and grim. Uncle Tony never really seemed to have a good answer for me about the spent fuel rods; they were working on it, though. But he always assured me that a nuclear meltdown was highly unlikely. Unlikely 'til now, when it's real.

The Civil Rights Movement. Vietnam. The Cold War. Apartheid. The trashing of our environment. The Rise of the Nuclear Age. The SALT Talks. The Nuclear

Arms Treaty. Passing the EPA. I grew up as an activist - listening, reading, writing letters, calling senators, marching, campaigning. What the fuck good did it do when the world can be destroyed by one mistake? Or one madman? Stills is in my head singing: " there's somethin' happenin' here..."

Getting into the van to head to Deering High School, I ask Meredith if she'd heard what happened; she did. We all did. After each show today we load up the van and cruise along silently. I'm switching stations to find the news on the radio. They keep interrupting the music and updating:

Two persons known dead... they have it contained......the Russians say it is; Europe's not so sure........Wind carrying fallout over parts of northern......

Oh, no, wait!
.....there's a problem with reactor number four- a second explosion- no known cause.....

Who the hell knows what's going on?

I'm in front riding shotgun. Shotguns seem quaint. If only the world was armed only with shotguns. I switch the station again. Springsteen's smoldering voice pining I'M ON FIRE. Yeah, man. The whole damn world is.

Tell The Truth. It's The Easiest Thing To Remember

No, that isn't what I said! You asked me what I thought.

Michael and I are lingering over now cold cups of coffee at HORSEFEATHERS on Middle Street, Portland, after another energizing rehearsal for Pinter's THE LOVER.

Yeah, but, you're so intense about it. You're intense.

What does that word even mean, Michael?! I am so sick of that admonition. Please explain to me what it means?

It's just that you're really present; you're the most authentic person I know. You are so honest. Sometimes, TOO honest.

Is that bad?

My coffee cup slams a bit too hard back into its saucer.

No, it's good. But people don't know how to handle it. I don't know how to handle it.

Driving back home on 95 to Ogunquit later, I wonder how many hours I have spent on this Maine Turnpike between Portland and Wells, Maine in all my time of rehearsing and performing. Four million years seems about right. But, mostly I'm thinking stuff like this:

Ohmygod!!! From now on I'll try to be more fake! What the fucking fuck??!!! Is "intense" "passion"? Tell me YOUR truth! Jesus. Challenge me! Argue with me! I really don't get people. I never said it was my way or the highway! Maybe I feel like everyone else is intense - or maybe just bland - or is it two-faced? Can people just grow the fuck up?!

What I would give to meet another authentic person. No wonder I feel like a stranger here. I don't get the game or the rules. Give me a stupid rule and I'll smash it to bits. Ugh. Alan Parsons Project staunching my tears. "I don't care what you do! I wouldn't want to be like you!"

 And what the heck is this about?
" Stathoplos Breathes Fire Into Callas Role"
"The exquisitely real Lisa Stathoplos...."
"....a chameleon who becomes her character"
Years and years of glowing theatre reviews in multiple publications. Then, conversations I overhear:

"......she blurs the lines between reality and art...."

Isn't that the point?
Audience members recognize me in the street:

"Oh, Lisa, I cried a river at the show last night!"
Yeah? You're flowing and I'm going down for the third time.

It's very rewarding and I appreciate the appreciation. But I take it with a few truckloads of NaCl. I'm starting to get it. You love my truth on stage but in life the truth is too much? So, reality in art - good! In real life? NO.

Maybe I oughta take a hard look at myself. Oh, wait! I've cracked more mirrors in self-reflection than most people glance at in a friggin' lifetime. And I own my shit. I'd like a chum. Who'll go right to the mat with me.

Oh, takin' a swipe, are you? Well, here's a left hook! Why won't you dance around with me in this crazy ring of life? On the balls of our feet and no gloves. NO HALF TRUTHS! No carefully worded exchanges! Just the straight on raw deal. The unvarnished truth. I can take it. You'll survive. We'll be closer. Sheesh! Wouldn't that be nice? A friggin' match made in heaven. Champs.

Best. Friend. Ever.

Who the hell is this bombshell?! Thought just before this moment: I hated directing classes and workshops at Orono; what the hell was I thinking, agreeing to direct here at Porpus Players? That is an honest to God real name that I will never firmly wrap my mind around but, there you have it.

My high school director and creative writing teacher, who I affectionately refer to now as "O'D", because we are friends, ropes me into a directing gig this summer for this weirdly named theater and I have chosen the work of one of the most difficult playwrights to master - Harold Pinter. BETRAYAL, no less. This afternoon I have fidgeted and mindlessly kicked my leg through the earnest monologues of a number of insufficient actresses deeply desirous of the role of Emma in this four-person gem and I am beginning to energetically fade when she walks in. Tall and slender with a halo of ravishing strawberry blonde hair backlit by the glow of the lowering sun at the River Club and I am thinking:

If she doesn't trip on stage and she mumbles the lines, she's getting the friggin' part.

She can say the lines. She can move. She will be my Emma. Hallafuckinlujiah. Saved by The Belle!

Hey, you wanna come over to my house in Perkins Cove to talk about the part?

She seems pleased, that's good.

I am making a pot of tea as she climbs the stairway to our second-floor apartment we share with six working girls in the summer. I long for privacy - and two bathrooms.

There is something about this young woman. I had been acquainted with her from afar in high school and, back then, she called herself "Sue" but now she goes by "Suze". I'm hearing and seeing "867-5309" scratched on a bathroom stall in my head and she can go by "Jenny" if she likes - I don't care. She used to shyly wave to me as we passed in the hallways between classes. She was a little eighth grader and I was a senior. She never failed to make me smile. There was just something about her.

Now, we just click. There is no better word. We feel the same things, love the same things, finish each other's sentences and thoughts and want to hang out, talk and laugh, eat Rolo candies, drink copious amounts of wine yet never be drunk and marvel at how we each got along without each other all these years. I have a best friend. A REAL, honest to goodness best friend and we are now inseparable in our spare time.

On stage in BETRAYAL, Suze positively glows as Emma. Her fellow actors are fine but Suze radiates light and nuance and maturity beyond her years. Our journey as best friends, theatrical colleagues and perfect foils for each other is launched. And, we are not afraid.

Suze is an amazing actor but directing and writing are her twin gifts. She has cast me as Babe in CRIMES OF THE HEART - same year I will do it at Portland Stage. Funny thing, that. See, companies have to acquire these pesky things called performance rights before they can mount shows. Crazy little notion that playwrights ought to be paid for their work. CRIMES is a new play by Beth

Henley and rights are typically not awarded to two companies within a certain proximity to each other especially when the play is new. So, when I show up to the table read for the same play at Portland Stage to be mounted that fall, imagine Barbara Rosoff's interest that I have just been riding the first weekend opening high as Babe in said play at Kennebunkport.

How did your company get the rights?

Gulp. Not my responsibility but, maybe I should mention this to the gang at PP. It doesn't go well. Apparently, Kim or Al or someone with official technical duties such as rights procurement had neglected to file the necessary paperwork. Fastest opening and closing of a smash hit in southern Maine theatrical history, I imagine.

I am getting close to leaving semi-professional theatre in my rearview; my training and ambition are hounding me: you are a serious actor.

Nowhere Men

Ugh. I do not want to make this phone call.

Sloan Lab Caltech, how can I help you?

Shit. I thought I had Jamie's dad's number.

Hello? Professor Birk?

No. Sloan Lab, honey. Who are you looking for?

Professor Birk? Ah, Doctor Birk; he's a physicist?

Uh, huh. We've got a lotta them here. Hold, please.

Days pass. Existential questions pop up. How many rocket scientists does it take to jumpstart a jet propulsion lab? Is it harder to get into MIT or Caltech? (Pretty sure it's MIT) How many quacks does it take to know a quark exists?

Deep voice.

Hello?

Hi, Dr. Birk, it's Lisa. Jamie's okay but he's um.... well, he is breaking all the rules and, I think it's time he went home...home to Pasadena.
Agonizing pause.

He can't come back here. His mother doesn't want him here.

Wow. Just like that. Done with a son. Todd and I invited seventeen-year-old Jamie to live with us last fall when he threatened to drop out of Wells High. He was my very first private acting student; I worked with him on the character of Tom in Williams' THIS PROPERTY IS CONDEMNED. He was so talented, good looking and smart - he had everything going for him. But, he couldn't stand living with his uncle whom he hated. I suspect the feeling was mutual; there was a reason Jamie got kicked out of his parents' house in Pasadena and was moved to the opposite coast. So he decided he could live on the streets. His next plan was to drop out of school.

I picked him up once on a rainy Wednesday to get him to his evening rehearsal. He was living under a blue tarp along the side of Route 109 near Sanford. Crap was lying around everywhere and the gutter next to his tarp tent was full of water. When cars passed at 50 mph, the tires spewed water and silt all over it. When he got into my Toyota Tercel he looked like a drowned rat. I made him a deal:

You can live with us and we will provide food, shelter and basics. BUT! You have to stay in high school. Big grin.

Okay. Thanks!

Megawatt smile.

I suspect he's gotten by on his charm a lot. Everything was great - for a while. Jamie had a room upstairs in our second-floor apartment which he kept neat, his grades were great and he was knocking it out of the park in the high school play as Danny Zuko in GREASE. Then, what little spare cash Todd and I had started to disappear. First from a kitchen change jar, then my purse and then Todd's wallet. I didn't want to believe it was Jamie, but it got more and more obvious. When I finally confronted him he denied knowing anything about the money. Sigh. We decided he needed an allowance and came up with something that seemed appropriate. Our money stayed put for a while. Then Jamie started disappearing - first for a night here and there and then for days at a time. Each time he returned I would sit and talk to him and ask him, please, to just let us know his plans.

Oh sure, of course, of course! I will.

Hmmmmm.

In July, Todd and I decided to take a rare overnight "vacation" to Aroostook County and perchance escape the creeping humidity in southern Maine. Maybe I subconsciously wanted to escape from Jamie too; I don't know.
We had a great time visiting my mom's French-speaking hometown on the Canadian border where she grew up on the family farm with her nine brothers and only sister. She learned English at age thirteen. We went past her house that seemed a bit worse for wear and canoed in Fish River. And, thankfully, escaped humidity for a bit.

On our return to Perkins Cove, Jamie is nowhere to be found. Nor is Todd's Chevy. The truck he uses to haul bait and cusk from Perkins Cove to Portland, Maine after tub-trawling 25 miles offshore every day. It's not a new truck but.....yeah.

Are you friggin' kidding me, Jamie??!!!!!!!

Screaming this in the driveway does not bring the truck or Jamie back. This time, we actually call the police. Jamie shows up with the truck days later. He casually hikes up the stairs to our apartment.

Get out.

His look of surprise is telling; he can't believe I am doing this.

Sorry! I promise I won't do it again!

That's right, you won't. You're out, Jamie. I'm sorry, but you have broken our trust too many times. I'm really sorry.

FUCK YOU!

And, after grabbing his few things upstairs:
SLAM. The front door shakes the house. And I shake and sob.

He's not the last troubled human I take in.
There's Fred, a few years older than me, who I met when I was eighteen and who, whenever he cruised into The Cove in his spiffy red Karmann Ghia sports car with the top down, we'd meet and sit on the rocks at Oarweed Cove or at Einstein's New York Deli and talk life's existential questions and philosophy for hours on end. He lives with us for a winter after he falls on hard times and stays until his demands on my time exceed my patience and stretch the limits of my kindness.

There's June, much older than me - an odd duck I meet on Ogunquit Beach - with her long puffy purple down coat and who has some secret wealth so she treats me to extraordinary dinners at Portland's finest restaurants like Brattle Street where we chat amiably about art and culture. But there is something off about her. She, too, teaches me about my limits when her demands on my empathy become wildly out of touch with what a working girl can accommodate and I need to push her away.

I take in my best friend who is struggling after life dealt her a harsh blow. She's a mess but she's my best friend; this time there's a better outcome.

We house another Jamie as a favor to a friend and he stays for a year. He is annoying as hell with his quirky oddities in our shared living space and his routines that must never be wavered from and his nearly robotic communication style. He very nearly severed my last nerve. Later on I realize he was a person likely on the spectrum of autism and I'm annoyed with myself for being annoyed with him. He was really very amusing and gentle if at times frustrating.

I take people in until we finally move from The Cove. But lost souls and lonely wanderers continue to find me.

My Spirit Guides

The next time I take someone in, she stays. A friend of Mom's said she really couldn't have her living with her anymore and asked Mom if I could take her in. Tired of adding random wayward folks to our abode, I agree only to meet her; she is living in Angel's garage. With her silky black hair and smokey green yellow eyes she is definitely stunning. And though she is skittish at first when she finally emerges and I wrap her in my arms it is kismet; she's coming home with me.

I name her Sassafras. She will be the first of an endless string of four-legged creatures I take in - dogs, cats, rabbits - always from shelters or others who wander to our home and find me. I have always found it easier to relate to animals than to people. Like me, they're direct and get right to the point - for better or worse. At least you always know where they stand. Sassafras, Dark Star, Sanchez, Sheepshank, Diesel start me on my way - the list will go on and on, I know this. Animals are so superior to humans. I have never bought that we are the sole owners of souls; in so many ways animals are more advanced than us. This sentiment is frowned upon in our culture and most definitely so by the Catholic Church. Oh well, good thing I left organized religion in my rearview long ago.

Wince! Phew, no lightning bolt yet, but, I'm guessing if there really is a Caucasian male God who's not into Animism, I'm on a watch list.

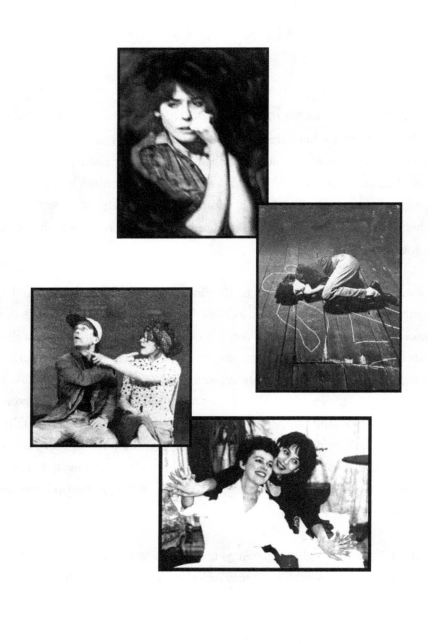

It's a Long Way To The Top

Michael Rafkin and I are lying in our bathing suits under a wool blanket on a freezing beach in Scarborough in early June between takes. VP Productions in Portland making the ad.

Take three!

Three? It seems more like three hundred at this point and I am questioning the morality of hawking J.N. Selleck jewelry and what the company's politics are. Anything to get us off this frigid beach. But, no, we say the lines, chat animatedly in between takes about what the Theatre means to us and laugh at the inanity of making commercials for products we couldn't care less about while simultaneously ticking off the check amount we'll be rewarded for the effort. We haven't met before but we know each other's work - he as a talented director and me as an actor. It is decided. We need to work together. Now, to the how.

This time we meet on Brown Street at Hu Shang's. Over wonton soup and spring rolls with crispy cold glasses of Chardonnay we nail down our mutual desire to form a new theatre company, designate a tiny selection of actors we will invite in and plot strategy. It is thrilling, heady and feels portentous. Michael is clearly brilliant, well-trained and very well-seasoned. In his cache of accomplishments post Carnegie-Mellon, is the venerable Profile Theatre company, now, Portland Stage Company. We do not want to be Portland Stage. We want to do edgy, challenging and in your face theatre - the kind most established companies must shy away from lest the board and their supporters abandon them in favor of what pleases the mainstream. In that world, conservatism rules.

Now, David Kraft is crouching inside a fireplace where I have just sprayed him with an entire can of Raid roach killer while whacking him with a fireplace poker and screaming obscenities after his attempt to rape me. It is the second act of Mastrosimone's EXTREMITIES and we are performing to sold out audiences at Luther Bonney Auditorium on the USM campus under the name Illuminati Productions. We are four actors with Michael directing. David survives due to clever Props Masters and ingenious choreography. In the audience tonight are two New York actors currently in A. R. Gurney's THE DINING ROOM at PSC. They are smitten. They want to meet and talk to us.

Great Lost Bear on Forest Avenue, Portland, 1985. Mad Horse Theatre Company is born with an opening season at The Theater of Fantasy, home to Tony Montanero and Celebration Mime Theatre on Danforth Street. We become the hot artistic property of Portland gaining immediate success with hard-hitting lesser-done plays and new works by our playwright-in-residence, Martin Jones. We do an all-female version of Israel Horowitz's THE INDIAN WANTS THE BRONX! Judith Thompson's THE CRACKWALKER is scheduled. Playing Beth in Jones' VANISHING POINTS, I know I have found my theatrical home with this ensemble and with my director, Michael. Our "simpatico" is so deep and palpable he rarely needs to finish a sentence before I nod and say, "got it!". We speak the same artistic language and feed off each other. I believe this company that I was integral in creating and helped to earn its early success is my forever home. We are critically acclaimed. We are Portland's darlings. Nothing could ever tear us apart. Could it?

"Oh! Darling, if you leave me, I'll never make it alone...." The Beatles cautioning in my head.

My training at Orono brought me to this dream theatrical home. I remember all of that training so well.

Sympathy For The Devil

No, no, no, no, no! Again!!!

Baritone voice from the very back of the house in Hauck Auditorium at UMaine/Orono. I fall off the imaginary railroad tracks I am walking as Willie in THIS PROPERTY'S CONDEMNED by Tennessee Williams and stand, dejected, gazing out off the stage into the darkness of the theater. Dr. James Bost, formidable and intense Scottish director, notorious amongst theatre majors for spending entire four-hour rehearsals on one page of Chekhov and reducing fragile ingenue wannabes to wracking sobs is putting me through my paces in my twice weekly, two-hour Advanced Acting Practicum session held between three and five o'clock on Tuesdays and Thursdays. My last nerve is threatening a snap.

Have you seen Jodie Foster in TAXI DRIVER?!

I have not, I am horrified to say - every single upperclassmen is gabbing about how brilliant De Niro is in it and I know Ms. Foster's depiction of the character of the young prostitute is being hailed as Oscar-worthy. I wish I was Jodie Fucking Foster and anywhere but in this demoralizing acting class and why did I decide to major in freakin' theatre anyway, what the fuck do I know about acting, I've never even heard of Uta freaking Hagen or Joe Papp or Strindberg or any of these supposed greats that all my classmates seem to know so well. In my head I have already switched to a double major in Forestry and Mechanical Engineering - notoriously the most difficult at UMaine - but nothing could be worse than the humiliation of a Theatre Arts degree. How hard could Forestry really be? Hey! I'm a Stumpie now! Forestry majors are called " Stumpies".

He's ON the stage now. Why doesn't HE just play the friggin' part if he's not gonna even give me a chance to get half a line out without stopping me?

So, apparently, Jodie Foster ought to be my model for Willie, what with her precocious world-weariness and ability to beguile and disarm. I exit stage left, take another deep breath and attempt the scene again. By the time five o'clock rolls around, I am always starving, always feeling like a bad actor and always determined to one day prove myself to Dr. Bost.

Jim Bost, Dr. James Bost or, Bost, to some, has been one of my four illustrious professors of theatre at UMaine/Orono for three years. For a Theatre Arts degree at Orono, in addition to acting classes, there are directing classes, British drama, American drama, lighting design, scene study, Commedia d'ell arte, stagecraft, voice, theories of acting, costume design, scene design, more acting classes and long, long rehearsals. He is impulsive, infuriating, terrifying, inspiring and, ultimately, because he is kind and clearly brilliant, he is the director whose approval I and so many theatre majors seek the most. He bristles. He snaps. He stops you mid vowel. We climb through Stanislavski and The Method, veer into Strasberg and The Actor's Studio, slide onto Meisner, happen upon Uta Hagen and HB Studios, cruise through Stella Adler, labor over Michael Chekhov and his psychological gesture and always, ALWAYS hammer on THE WORK to find EMOTIONAL TRUTH in acting. Well, yeah. No shit, Sherlock. But, THE WORK with Jim Bost is grueling and without sentiment. Work with Dr. Bost requires steel, commitment, guts, tenacity and, behind his back, a lot of tears.

James Bost is famous for leaping onstage during rehearsals for major productions all scarlet-faced, his thick, graying red hair parted on the side falling wildly like a curtain across his face as he strides willy-nilly around the stage demonstrating the way the scene should be played and all the while quoting lines by saying things like, "then Sonya does talkity talkity talk talk talk "tell me the whole truth, Astrov"" and talkity talkity talk talk and Sonya implores "What can we do? We must live our lives" and hands Vanya the samovar and Astrov says "I am exhausted, Sonya, and I rush over here and I am tired and talkity talkity talk talk talk" and on like that.

He was doing this one time during cast notes at the end of a long evening rehearsal for O'Neill's A TOUCH OF THE POET while the entire cast sat scribbling notes furiously about three quarters back from the lip of the stage and then watched in silent horror, fascination and bizarrely dumbstruck as Doctor James Bost "talkity talked" his way backward to the very edge of the thrust stage and fell three feet down to the orchestra pit, apparently onto his back. We didn't know; we could not see him. Abject silence and stillness ensued - such was the terror and thrall he held over his students.

I contemplated how and if an accessory to murder charge would hinder my future acting prospects as I pictured him lying twisted and swollen on the ruby red pile carpet of Hauck Auditorium, neck turned at an awkward angle, legs askew, while his dying gasps rasped vainly out of him - no help on the way - and we all remained absolutely stationary in a kind of dark and retributional theatrical tableau when, at last, one freckled ham of a hand grasped the lip of the stage, then the familiar green, black and blue of his classic Black Watch Tartan plaid shirt-sleeve rolled to the elbow appeared as he drew his remarkably limber fortysomething self back up onto the stage, seemingly unscathed but nonetheless a bit rattled and, perhaps, a touch sheepish. Then, fixing all of us in his most penetrating glare, he stated:

Not a word about this to ANYONE, you hear?

It was all over campus by the following morning.

Senior year, after three shows and numerous classes with this impossible yet brilliant director, I have him wrapped around my finger as an actor and he is thrilled with my work. He demonstrates this by the twinkle in his eye when I nail a performance. BUT! There is always more work to do. That sense of an actor's work never being done is ingrained in me thanks in no small part to Doctor James Bost.

Bye Bye Route 66

Let's get this crap packed up and get outta here! Where are we next? Searsport?

Tim, unbuckling a flat while I hastily fold and wrap Juliet's Elizabethan-style dresses. It's 9:45 in Caribou, Maine and we still have two more shows today and hundreds of miles before we get back to The Theater at Monmouth and sleep. It's been a long touring season and we are all exhausted. High school gyms are our typical venue in these parts; southern Maine has more schools with actual auditoriums. Doesn't matter, our ROMEO AND JULIET can go up anywhere.

Can I talk to you?

An older man in overalls, exuding the slightest whiff of hay, approaches me. He runs his hand over the top of his thinning grey hair.

Hi! Sure, sure, thank you for coming to the show.

I never ever saw nothin' like that! It seemed so REAL and I understood all of it even though it's Shakespeare. I wasn't gonna come but my daughter in high school here said I should.

Wow, this lovely and humble potato farmer has tears in his eyes - holy shit!

Oh, good, good. Yeah, some people think Shakespeare is hard to understand but it shouldn't be! We are so glad you enjoyed the show and thank you so much for coming by to talk to us.

He thanks us all again and lopes away. I know I will not forget this moment in Caribou, Maine. It is the moment I know why I choose to remain a regional working actor. We don't all gravitate to New York or LA. I certainly don't. Because I think everyone deserves access to high quality live theatre no matter where they live. Talented people, artists, are everywhere. I know this because I live this. Please don't ask me why I stay in Maine. Or New England. Please stop telling me to go to New York. I hate the American star system and its worship of celebrity - it's so adolescent. I trained to be an actor at Orono and have never stopped training: voice classes, advanced acting classes, technique, scene study. A friggin' year of Meisner. All that and the everyday work of observing human behavior - something I've done since I was a kid. I do what I do because it calls to me and feels like home. I like visiting cities but I could never live in a big one; they make me feel hopeless and lost. Portland, Maine is a good size. It is my home and has talent galore. There is nothing like live theatre.

Nights In White Satin

I can feel Candace Morton's breath under my raised left arm as she sews me into my 20s style white satin antique flapper dress in the 6 by 12 dressing room of Mad Horse Theatre. Neither of us say a word. The forced intimacy of this moment is mind boggling. No one in the company has spoken to me in one month and we do five shows weekly. On opening weekend I resigned from the company due to what the papers called "irreconcilable differences". I am finishing the run of this show only. I feel I cannot go on with the company after a defining incident that made the decision to leave awful but inexorable. I will just say that things got very ugly over something that felt untenable to me and I no longer trusted Mad Horse. My heart and soul and sweat and tears went into co-founding this company; resigning broke my heart.

So, here we are. No one talking to me in the last week of a sold out run of Alejandro Sieveking's PRAYING MANTIS with critics falling all over themselves. We are on again in five as crazy sisters Lina and Llalla for the Act II wedding scene. No wardrobe person is available for this task and my dress fits so precisely and is so delicate, this sewing in must be done every show. Only Candace is available. Her closeness kills me. Sometimes I want to scream. Sometimes I want to laugh out loud. I wonder if she'll prick me with the needle and then say I'm sorry. Sometimes I want to punch this talented actress I love working with right in the face. Artists' squabbles. Artists' jealousies. I feel like this. You feel like that. Whatever. We aren't the friggin' Eagles but, it's not looking like we'll have our version of the When Hell Freezes Over Tour anytime soon. She ties the knot and leans into my left ribs, exhales, and bites the thread off with her teeth. Despite all, I want to embrace her.

Why won't you talk to me? What the FUCK is wrong with you? I say nothing. Hey, maybe, like, twenty-five years from now we'll share a stage again. My thoughts float off.

Turns out, I'm clairvoyant.

First rehearsal, AUGUST: OSAGE COUNTY by Tracey Letts at Good Theater, Portland. Twenty-five years later.

Hey, Candy!

She hates being called Candy. I've always gotten away with it though - one of only two people who do. I know how she feels about me as an actor; that has never changed. The mutual respect gets us through the hard part.

Hey, there, girl, how the hell are ya?

Good. Long time no see.

There's an understatement. The water flowing under my Mad Horse shitshow took the bridge out with it years ago. Funny. We are playing sisters again. Something feels very right about that.

Today Mad Horse Theatre is in its thirty fifth season.

Freak Show

Knowing I am deformed is something I carry with me always.

It is not about my spine; that is handily hidden by clothing most of the time and looks much straighter than it once did. Mom used to routinely have me lift the back of my shirt so she could trace her caring fingers over each of my tortured vertebrae to see my progress. I can feel her hands trace the bump, bump bump, down from my neck and then, slightly to the right, then a LOT to the right and on down to the left hook my spine takes at the base of my back. A casual observer might not notice the bones of my spine. But Mom always saw. She always knew. Today my back has definition and musculature that may be uncommon for most women but years and years and hundreds and hundreds of specific exercises later are visible evidence of a hard-won battle with a congenital malformation.

No, I am deformed because I have always been pretty flat-chested. The taunts on the bus were more scathing and hurtful because, unlike standard run-of-the-mill ignorant bullying, I knew them to be true. Now I hear about it from casual thoughtless comments - sometimes even friends who tease and the one lover who said something hurtful. Gary Kilgore after our first crazy love-making session on the eighth floor of the Trelawny Building in Portland, Maine:

I didn't take your dress off completely because I thought you'd be embarrassed.

Oh, wow, thanks. It never ever occurred to me to be embarrassed. Number, let's see, how many lovers am I up to now? Number....ten? No man before you ever seemed to have any trouble finding me deliciously beguiling or mentioned anything wrong with my anatomy. What the fucking fuck? Oh, and, by the way, sorry about your dick.

Of course, I believe I am head over heels in love with this paean to self-absorption. Maybe a coupla decades from now I'll know surpassing intimacy in all its manifestations: physical, emotional and spiritual. For now, just dump this dude.

And then there's the husband of a long-time friend notorious for copping a feel whenever opportunity knocked. I'll call him "Dan". One wild dance party at Dan and Gail's house, Dan glides over to grab me for some swing dancing. While he's shuffling his feet and managing to roam my body with his wayward hands he says:

It doesn't make any sense. You take all the parts alone and it isn't much but, somehow, put it all together and it works.

Heavy breathing and sigh.

Thanks? I guess? Why does that not feel like a compliment?
Interestingly, none of my female friends nor I hate this man. There's a thing that makes no sense.

I have developed a strategy to undercut the possibility of people's unintentionally callous words or thoughts cutting or embarrassing me: I beat people to the punch by noting my deformity before they can say anything. "No, I would never wear that - too flat-chested!" "Oh, I never have to worry about a running bra - no problem there. Ha, ha!" Bam. Problem solved. Don't worry, people. I already know what I look like so you don't need to tease me or point it out.

Here's a little secret. I have been having people stop me for some time now on the street or as I walk Shore Road or sit on the steps to the Norseman Motel at Ogunquit Beach and say things like, "you are absolutely beautiful." (from a quite stunning fortyish woman) or, "you should be a model." (A French-Canadian man on Main street in front of Tower Drug) I know - weird, right? I can't say this doesn't feel sort of good but, I know it is not true and I know if they think it is then there is something very wrong with them.

I do have a style all my own now and I am not talking about worn out jeans and a tie-dye t-shirt with an oversize jean jacket. I like lots of different clothes now. I wear cool and breezy East Indian dresses and skirts that I mix with black fitted jackets or filmy blouses that don't cling but look ephemeral and easy. I don't like anything too complicated or contrived - no belts, my only jewelry dangly or hoop earrings and the necklace from my Uncle Pat that I never take off. My straight dark hair is waist-length and thick with blonde highlights from summer days spent on a beach or a boat. I wear a lot of hats; they look good on me, especially berets and fedoras. The berets assist in me being stopped by Customs agents at airports and in various countries' Border Security checkpoints pretty much always. Thanks, Patty Hearst.

My favorite time this happened - there are so many, really - is returning to the U.S. after another fabulous trip to Quebec City with Todd.

On this occasion the trip is a bit dampened by my head cold whose predominant feature was a runny nose that produces copious amounts of mucus. As we approach the U. S. border heading back to Jackman, Maine, I have completely exhausted the ready supply of trash receptacles for sopping wet Kleenex and have quite a mountain of the used rags piling at my feet. American flag flat out in a stiff northwest breeze and the car slows. A notably large female American agent saunters heavily toward our Datsun 5-10 with the classic blue and white NO NUKES sticker on the rear window. I stuff some stray hairs into my Grateful Dead "Steal Your Face" crocheted beret.

Customs agents on the U. S. side of the border are almost cartoonishly different from their counterparts on the Canadian side. When entering Canada, an almost always good-looking Canadian male sidles out of his drab, minimalistic government building with the cheerful maple leaf Canadian flag waving and approaches the car with an impish smile.

Bonjour! Comment ca va?

Bien, merci! Et vous?

Ah, oui, bien aussi! Ou va allez?

A Quebec.

Passports are glanced at, backseats are cursorily perused.

Avez-vous les pommes o les oranges?

No, no! No fruit.
Bien sur! Bienvenue! Bon voyage!

And we happily trundle on.

The U. S. gang is a bit different. Always a humorless bunch but, this particular time, more fun than usual. My beret adjusted, Mrs. U.S. finally reaches the car and begins her robotic rote questioning in an impressive monotone:

Passports.

We dutifully hand them over.

What are your names?

Wow. Seems like the passports would've been a dead giveaway.

Where do you live?

You're making me so fucking nervous I don't remember anymore.

How long have you been in Canada?

I don't know but now I'm wishing we stayed.
Opens the hatchback and hauls out my eighteen-thousand-pound yellow Samsonite suitcase. Clips the latches and rummages. Underwear everywhere. Smushes up my harem pants and wrinkles them. Finds my EpiPen. I carry it for years now since I started having choking fits where my throat closes completely and I cannot breathe. Allergist Dr. Pennoyer of Vaughn Street in Portland prescribes it to me and recommends I carry it always.
Mind Numbingly Dull Voice cracks the air again.

What is THIS?

I explain. On a face that has registered little as of yet, something resembling disbelief fleets by. She eyes me with suspicious scrutiny. I admit, I eye her BACK. That does it, I guess.

Get out of the car.

This a first and I am pretty sure a strip search involving the usual grisly details will now ensue. She begins to completely, no, really, COMPLETELY tear the car apart beginning with my suitcase, every loose object in it, then the floor mats, the spare tire hold, the dashbox, under the hood and everything not bolted down. But. What made this blood-cooling episode worth it was the used Kleenex. Mrs. U. Friggin'. S. picked up Every. Single. Snot Filled. Rag. and pulled its viscous, virus filled contents open searching for I know not what? Cocaine mush?

I start giggling hysterically as Todd and I watch helplessly while sitting on the curb of the U.S. Customs facility in Jackman, Maine. I cannot stop; I laugh uncontrollably, certain we are about to face years of detention in a Fort Kent jail a la the Hollywood blockbuster Midnight Express. I cannot stop finding this freakishly hilarious. Todd is not amused. Mrs. Humorless U.S. finally concedes that we are not an internal threat to the contiguous United States by virtue of professing our opposition to the proliferation of nuclear power or my curious resemblance to Patty Hearst. She reluctantly throws the EpiPen back in my suitcase. We chuck it in the back hold without restuffing it or clasping it and head back home. But our thoughts remain back in Canada. Hmmm. Canada.

I am now an accomplished actor and dancer and I am comfortable in my own skin. I am routinely measured and dressed by countless designers and makeup artists for the stage and for the wealth of industrial film and independent film that I now secure for excellent legal tender. Even here, though, I have encounters with personnel who somehow manage inadvertently to reopen the age-old wound of feeling not quite right physically.

Merle, much sought-after New England based make-up artist, pulling blouses from JCPenney for my umpteenth Levinsky's television commercial shoot and yanking the curtain to my dressing room once mid-strip and exclaiming:

Wow! You look just like a teen!

I want to die. Why do I even do this stupid work? Oh, yeah, dumbass - the money.

To this day there is no way I will wear certain items and no way do I ever want to undress in front of anyone. Finding the right shirts is an essential task. No, I don't want or need your help or your comments of what looks good on me. Only I know what I feel comfortable in and what looks good. An exception to this rule might be my sister, Karen, who always manages to find me camisoles and shirts and blouses I like. Mom, too. I have been blessed with long, shapely legs and thinness so I get a lot of this:

"You have such a dancer's body!"
"You can wear anything. Everything looks great on you!"
Slim hips, long arms and lankiness help with that. But those comments won't fix my deformity. Sometimes I want to hit people back and get them in their Achilles' heels - you know, where it could really hurt, like, "nooooooo, I don't think it's the pants..." "Maybe you outta rethink that dress..." or, "Have you considered higher education? Reading?" but I never do. I try not to talk about

people's bodies (or their minds...) unless they bring up some concern. I marvel sometimes at all the major roles I have played thus far - ingenues from Juliet to Miranda. Maggie the Friggin' Cat! How on earth did I pull off that icon of sensuality when so unshapely?! The reviews raved again. Yeah, I pulled it off.

Here's a weird thing. Even as I know I am deformed and you cannot convince me otherwise to this day, the paradox is: I kind of know I am not deformed. Society, this culture is deformed, not me. I am just a variation on countless human physiological themes. Still, it hurts.

I have had moments when I tasted what being slightly buxomy is like. And. I. Hated. It. Being pregnant helps breasts to fill out and nursing continues the trend. The longest I have nursed is six months with my son, Luke. I like the idea of the closeness of mother and child that nursing brings but, honestly, having another human latched onto my body - especially a part that I have accepted as not normal - is not my favorite thing and I am relieved when I no longer need to lift my milk-stained shirt every few hours to keep someone I love alive. And I am even more relieved when the fullness that was my alien chest returns to a comfortable thinness and my clothes hang the way they always have. Having a human lamprey attached to me? Even one I love more than my own life? Not so much.

A Horse Latitude With No Name

I'm lying on the foredeck of Swan Song, a 49-foot ketch Todd and I are crewing for Captain Clay Phillips, from St. Thomas, U.S. Virgin Islands, back to Perkins Cove, Maine. Todd's dad got us this gig. Clay and his beautiful, REALLY beautiful wife, Danny, own The Piping Plover on Pine Hill North in Ogunquit and I dance there all the time. They have fun dance bands like Lex and Joe and it's friggin' great. Clay is a well-known character in Ogunquit, sailing many vessels from Maine to the Virgins and only losing a couple. He and Danny are reputed to have a more fluid than solid relationship. Well, maybe it's solid in its fluid way. Either way, it seems like a gas.

It is my first time delivering a sailboat and I am completely green. People with money who own yachts often hire a crew to sail their vessels between some point in Maine or New England down to the U.S. or British Virgins or the French or Dutch West Indies so that they may fly in on their whims and sail around the clutter of islands in these places. In the spring they need those vessels returned to Maine harbors. There are two routes: the Intercoastal Waterway - hugging the coast all the way - or the offshore route, the Atlantic shipping lanes, with one landfall, Bermuda. The Intercoastal route means you are never far from a port; the offshore route means you are about 600 miles off the U.S. mainland and weather can be less predictable. The return trip from St. Thomas, U.S. Virgins to Ogunquit, Maine, with good weather, should take two weeks. I am invited along not for my sailing prowess but because I am Todd's wife. In fact, just two months ago Todd and I celebrated a belated honeymoon in Bermuda and we loved it.

There are five of us on board: Clay, the Captain; Peter, the cook; Larry Dick (yup) Local Harbormaster; Todd and me. Todd and his family are brilliant captains and seamen. Too bad he is not the captain now.

We're two days out of Bermuda. In the past week and a half I have learned a bit about offshore ocean sailing. There are the squalls that come up so suddenly that nicely making way with a following sea changes in a second to the starboard rail buried, sails frantically dropped, halyards screaming and us hiked out high on the port side. Then there's the startling flying fish who mistakenly land on deck in the middle of a peaceful, starlit night watch where the heavens truly teem with tiny points of endless light. There is learning to pee at a 45 degree angle in the tiny head when close-hauled and cruising and, there is learning to decipher the navigational lights of distant ships on the horizon to discern their position and headway on my 2 to 6 am lonely night watch - something I never learn to trust myself with. Oh, and halyard rides! Attaching the bosun's chair to the mainsail halyard when heeled hard over, climbing in, swinging out over the rail and smashing through the water while underway. A bit crazy, six hundred miles from land, but fun! I also learn that Captain Clay has trouble locating Bermuda. Just three passes and we finally find it. Interesting.

I also learn about sailors, all men, who sail completely naked. Not Todd. But, all the others all the time with their stupid dicks flapping in the breeze like they're proud. Huh. I'm 23 and naive about toxic males despite life experiences that should have informed me. Larry Dick's dick has a bumble bee tattooed on it. A fucking bumble bee. He probably thinks he's witty. I think he's aptly named. He likes to stand astride the companionway - the hatch with steps leading down below - where I read Marion Zimmer Bradley's latest at the settee by the bottom rung, and present it to me. Glancing up, I see it and picture it -

a shriveled, small and bloody quivering mass - lying on deck where I just lopped it off, his grimace of agony frozen in time. I smile, return to the page and drift back into THE MISTS OF AVALON.

Waking from my delicious nap up forward following our 2 to 6 am watch, I turn and glance astern to see if Todd is on deck.

Oh. My. God.

If there were a picture entry for "impending doom" in the dictionary, the sky behind us is what you would see. From horizon to horizon it is the pitchest black I have ever seen. My preternatural sense tells me this is coming for us and that it will NOT be good. I hate being right all the time. Wind starts to yowl and seas build in minutes. We scramble to drop sail and the boat is tossed like a Clorox bottle. The fiberglass Morgan is being battered badly. Clay's first reckless decision:

Todd, secure the Zodiac on the foredeck.

A Zodiac is a good-sized inflatable used to shuttle people and goods back and forth to the dock while anchored in port. It is quite heavy. Its stern is up against the jib stay like it's standing on its head. I watch Todd, catlike, navigate his way up forward, all the while we're taking green water over the rails, the decks are awash and, I know if he makes one slip and is overboard, no way could we ever get him back aboard in these conditions. I learn later that this was entirely foolhardy on Clay's part and a tether or safety line should have been attached to Todd before this maneuver.
What an asshole.

Within an hour or so the tops are being blown off the mountainous seas, estimated by all to be at thirty feet already. It's hard to judge at sea, but they are towering above the masts. Clay shouts above the din of the shrieking wind and pounding seas that it's time to go down below. We slide the companionway hatch shut just as we take a wave into the hold. Everyone and everything is soaked. Now we are just sitting ducks riding out a storm. 600 miles off Hatteras. In the Atlantic shipping lanes. What could go wrong?

Second stupid Clay decision: Todd tells me we should have put out something called a "sea anchor", a device towed astern that helps keep the bow headed up into the seas instead of taking them all broadside as we are now. Every wave slamming us feels like it will crack us in half. Nerves are on edge and we've all been awake for 36 hours before Clay tells us we need to sleep in shifts. He orders Todd and I to go first. We climb into the forward cabin exhausted and, despite all, we drop off almost immediately.

Slam!

Holy shit!!! Tooooodddddd!!! The starboard side is caved in!

I'm standing in seawater up to my knees and screaming.

Todd shoves me aside and grabs the porthole with one hand and slams it shut, then rips something off the stowaway cupboard with his right hand and yells at me.

It's the porthole, Lise ; it's just the porthole. Get a hammer!

Peter is now in the cabin and the two secure the busted porthole latch. It's the first time on this voyage that I really lose it. Now I am wondering for real if we are gonna get out of this. SWAN SONG may live up to its name.

Sitting around the settee while we slam around, every wave torturing the hull and us, we eat granola bars and stale bread. Peter can't cook on the gimbal stove - it's practically upside down all the time. No one is really hungry anyway. We listen to the marine radio. We can hear a ship somewhere - hopefully in the distance, because the chances of an ocean freighter bearing down on us and seeing and avoiding our little sailboat in the whiteout seas are just about nil. A couple somewhere out there on a demasted sailboat is hailing for help.

Mayday! Mayday!

One of them is hurt; we can't hear all of it. Jesus. What are we frickin' doing out here?! A lot of other things go wrong including a fire in the hold, which causes me to mutiny and scream at Clay. He sits doing nothing as the fire crawls up the galley wall.

What the fuck?! Put it out!!!!!

I picture our burned bodies drowning six hundred miles offshore in a maelstrom. I'm pretty sure my parents are gonna be bummed.
Clay, ever nonchalant.

It's just an alcohol fire. Water will put it out.

THEN FUCKING PUT IT OUT!!!!!!!!

What the fuck is wrong with this man?! Three days later - we've been hove to for THREE DAYS in a Hatteras storm that blew us hundreds of miles off course - and the wind is finally backing to the Westerlies. The seas are down enough for us all to emerge on deck. The clouds are breaking up and the sky is pale blue, orange and purple. There is sun. And hope. The seas are still huge; riding down a trough and then coming back up over the crest, we are all startled by a black and orange tanker passing on our port side literally about 50 yards away! Fifty yards in the shipping lanes is not cool. Holy shit. Again.

Back home, Dad, ever vigilant, has been watching the New York Times weather maps for Cape Hatteras and knows about this storm and rightly predicts we are in it. He does not tell Mom. We are a week overdue. It is the early eighties and there is no Internet and we do not have an international radio aboard. I'm never getting on a boat again with a captain I don't know and trust. We cannot wait to get off this boat.

The rest of the voyage is mercifully less eventful other than having to endure Clay's surpassing ignorance of all things having to do with good seamanship. He cannot navigate - forget dead reckoning; he can't properly use Loran. A day and a half from Perkins Cove we climb on deck after a long midnight watch to hear Clay's announcement.

We've just passed The Isles of Shoals!

Todd says nothing but disappears below deck. I feel excited. The Isles of Shoals means we are HOME! We sail in these waters all the time! Todd, in the companionway, nods to me. I go below. He always reworks Clay's figures because they are always wrong.

That wasn't The Shoals; that was Nantucket.

Fuckin A.

Nantucket isn't too far from home but we have more steaming to do. A day later, jubilation on the Finestkind dock. Our families are happy to see us. My Dad is really happy. They don't know what we went through yet. I'm glad we are out of the shipping lanes and back on dry land - no burns, no drowning. Yup. That would have really bummed them out.

Wish You Were Here

Ooooooowwwwwwwww!
My feet are scrunched up to my chest and my seatbelt is not clasped and this descent feels way too fast.

Lise, what is it?! What is happening?
Karen is terrified in the seat next to me.

I can't talk. My eye is going to explode. I've never felt a stabbing pain like this. The word in my mind is "excruciating". Tears are streaming down my face. The stewardess is absolutely no help - doesn't even suggest it's the sudden drop in air pressure that is causing it and I don't think of this. I can't think; the pain is blinding.

Ohmygodohmygodohmygod. I have my hand smashed into my right eye trying to quell the pain radiating through my whole head. The captain told us that we are over Athens and descending from 38,000 feet; he didn't mention he was going to do it in record time. My brain is gonna burst; this is too much. Even though we are coming down too fast it feels like an eternity until the familiar first bump and squeal of wheels hitting runway and then airplane hitting reverse. The pain goes on but lessens slightly. It makes me dizzy and disoriented. Taxiing into the airport, I quietly cry.

My sister and I are on our long-awaited trip to my Yaya and Papou's homeland following my graduation from Orono. We will spend two weeks with Greek relatives in Athens and Kalamata we have not yet met.

197

I'm thinking: When it comes time to leave, I just need to find a boat to sail home 'cause there's no fuckin' way I am getting on a plane again. Shouldn't be too hard: Mediterranean Sea to the Strait of Gibraltar, on through the Canaries, and then a straight shot across the Atlantic. That's my plan and I obsess on it. But I keep it to myself.

I am not a brilliant traveler; I know this. But, having just had an abortion almost 12 weeks into an unwanted pregnancy, planning a shotgun wedding two months from now with an empty friggin' shotgun and leaving behind my true love with my hormones in a deep dive doesn't help my mood. Poor Karen. She has always put up with so much from her moody, rebellious sister and now we are alone in Greece and she is the only one who speaks any of the language. Well, she won't mind taking the plane home alone; she's a really seasoned traveler. I'll let her know as soon as I secure passage on a tanker.

Passing the signs on the drive from the airport to our Aunt Mina and Uncle Demetrius's house where we will stay in Athens for our first week, all I can think is:

It's Greek to me!
The words don't just look foreign - they look alien. Whole different alphabet! Well, that and:

Holy crap, pollution!!!!

It is 1980 and Greece is a bit behind the U.S. in cleaning up its environment; the Parthenon is being eaten by smog and the Acropolis is often completely shrouded. It's a bit disappointing after all the amazing photographs in art and travel books and Vincent Hartgen's wild rants about the beauty of the ancient cultures of the world as he raved standing atop a desk and waving his arms madly during his legendary eight o'clock Art History class at Orono.

The relatives have learned of our arrival and all seven hundred of them meet us for our first dinner with Aunt Theresa and Uncle Sotiros intown Athens and, boy, do we eat. The Greeks want to feed you and feed you again and when you are full they must feed you some more. There can never be too much food at a Greek table. I know this from my Greek American relatives; their Greek counterparts would make their tables look stingy. It's a challenge because I do not eat a lot and Karen must constantly explain why I cannot eat more. Being thin doesn't help; this is a deeply perplexing sign to my Greek relatives who believe it is a sign of my imminent demise. They make it their mission to intervene.

What? An empty plate! Spanakopita!

More dolmathes! And Retsina!

Kala! For dessert, kourabiedes!

There is no getting through to them that I am not in danger. Argh. Tonight we have our own mini United Nations at table. We are speaking five languages because not all speak both Greek and English. So, Portuguese, French, Spanish and, of course, Greek and English are spewing in a great and boisterous table of Babel. I can manage the Spanish and Portuguese as they are similar and I understand a lot of French; Karen and Sotiros speak Greek and French and Mina struggles with her broken English.

Yasoo! Tee kahnis?

Kala. Efharisto! Kesis?

Vous avez une bon maison....

Es muy bonito, sí.....

Obrigado! Muito prazer em conhecê-lo!

Yo también.
Sí, sí, tengo mucho hambre....pero no es necessita....ah, no más, por favor!

Thelete ena bira? Krasi?

Efharisto, thank you, thank you...

Kronya pola!
Su viaje? ¿Está bien?

Ne, kalo taxithi.

Karen, what did you just say?

I just told her we had a good trip.

What are you kidding, Karen? Como se dice "the landing from hell"?

Shush, Lise.

America is good, no?

No. NO! Yes! Is good! Kala!

It is a happy chaos.

By the time Karen and I tumble into our shared bed at Mina's we barely hit the pillows before we are out. The memory of the landing lingers. I dream of sailing ships.

A week later, after a harrowing and uncomfortable nine-hour train ride through the Pelopponese reminiscent of Odysseus' return from Troy, we survive somehow and arrive at ten at night in Kalamata to stay with cousins Nikki and John in their beautiful country house by the sea. They have farmyard animals everywhere - goats and hens and horses and sheep. And turkeys. It is absolutely idyllic. We are exhausted and just want to fall into a bed but John has other things in mind.

Perfect! It is just time for dinner!

He exclaims excitedly. He will just pop out back and murder a turkey, roast it to perfection, and, in a mere two hours we'll sit down at midnight for a feast fit for kings. At midnight. Ugh. I know it is rude not to eat so I struggle through some feta and salad and Kalamata olives. But, roast turkey - especially a turkey whose unsuspecting self was happily roaming the yard just hours ago? At midnight? Oh, Greece, you are beautiful but you are nuts!

When we finally are led to our lovely sky blue room and throw ourselves on our backs amidst the soft and cool white cotton blankets, we sigh happily and glance up. We shriek in hysterics. We clutch each other and nearly choke to death from suppressed gales of laughter. Our sides are splitting. The ceiling is a reproduction, done fairly well, actually, of Michelangelo's paintings on the Sistine Chapel - fat cherubs with chubby fingers, angry gods in gathering clouds and all. Spent, finally, and still grinning inanely, we sleep.

We traipse on to Delphi where Apollo must have clammed up Pythia the Oracle for the day, damn him - no pithy prognostications for us - so I call her a fraud as I leap down from one of the ancient stones I am trespassing on and we continue our trek. I hope I haven't pissed off another god; they've got a lot of 'em here. I glance over my shoulder. They could gang up.

It is so hot it could melt our not yet dead flesh but we feel we will die without a drink of water or soda, even. We both hate soda. The only thing to be had in the small mountainside cafe is pear nectar. Pear nectar is basically melted lard sweetened with four hundred pounds of sugar. Or, at least at first sip. We choose dehydration.

Back in Athens we head down to Piraeus where we board a ferry with the rest of humanity - no, really, the ENTIRE HUMAN RACE is on this boat, to head to the island of Naxos. Only eight hours away with a crush of humans so pushy and boisterous climbing all over its three decks at their whim and with not one life jacket in sight sends Karen and me into fits of hysterics yet again. Hours later when I describe my trip to the only "head" aboard - it being a hole in the deck with urine and god knows what sloshing everywhere as you pee - she chooses not to pacify her bladder until we dock. She's no fun. I stay on deck and lust after passing freighters, my ticket home. They are my ticket home.

We fly home together. No freighter, nor tanker now can bear me hence.

Our lives diverge. I marry. She moves away to distant cities. Even apart, from here on, I fly with my sister - Teller of stories, Fellow aspiring artist, Mischievous playmate, Unalloyed Reverer of irreverent humor - she is my champion, my guiding light, my sense of equilibrium on an unstable planet always. Whether she likes it or not. The bond has been forged and it shall not be broken.

Mother Superior Jumps The Gun

It was bound to happen. I enter the convent. Yes, the High God of Comedy, if there is one, is dying of laughter while somersaulting off his throne. But, there really is no other choice for me.

Sister Marie (MY saint's name? You can't make this shit up...) leads me down the echoey corridor to the novitiate's meeting room. The Mother Superior awaits me for my preliminary interview.

"How do you solve a problem like Maria?" is on repeat in my head in a kind of taunting loop. In my typical reaction to all things Catholic, I am getting giddy. I struggle to swallow a rising guffaw. Can throats sustain hernias?

Welcome, Lisa! Welcome, child!

Mother Superior appears in a voluminous flowing habit doing an admirable impression of Peggy Wood in Robert Wise's THE SOUND OF MUSIC. I'm at 166 State Street, Portland, Maine and I swear I can smell edelweiss.

Hi. I mean....um.
Weird curtsy.

Hello! Madame. Ma'am? Reverend Mother?

Shit!!!!! How the frig are you supposed to address them?????
Thank you so much for meeting with me.

It means a lot. To me.

I wonder what to do with my hands. I grin inanely and awkwardly place them in "prayer mode". What the hell do you say to nuns?! I suppress an image of "here's the church and here's the steeple..." My hands open weirdly and all the people are showing. I jam them back in my coat pockets. Graciously, she offers me one of two yellow cushioned Queen Anne style chairs. There's a kneeler in front of mine. We sit to chat.

Oh, wow. Really? Only five years before final vows? Fascinating!

Ohmyfrigginword. Postulants make vows of three to five years?! Maybe we should try dancing! Reading Nabokov? What the hell am I doing here????!!!!!!

Lisa? Are you alright, my child?

The austere walls are closing in. Huh? What?! Where am I?!
What the fuck am I doing in here???!!!! I was only kidding!!!!!!
GETMETHEHELLOUTTAHERE!!!!!
Startled out of disassociating, I say all this in my head only, while the Mother Superior placidly recites epically long paths to nunhood.

Owwwww!

I bash my ankle bone on the kneeler in my attempt at a quick escape.

Of course, until you are a postulant, you have not yet committed to a life of Christ.....

Oh, right! I am learning about becoming a nun for my upcoming role in Pielmeier's AGNES OF GOD! I thought I had slipped into the seventh circle.

This is what being a serious dramatic actor is for me - what years of training taught me to do: my homework. I have spent weeks hanging out around a schizophrenic homeless woman in Deering Oaks, listened with specialized headsets to what the horror of voices in your head can mean, spent two days completely blindfolded to get a sense of a recent loss of sight and learned to play four chords on guitar. Years from now, I will study Maria Callas for two years before attempting Terrence McNally's MASTER CLASS and study addiction for over a year before I set foot into a rehearsal for Lett's AUGUST: OSAGE COUNTY. This diligence is long ingrained in me by professors and artists who taught me: Do your work. Respect the craft.

...and, Lisa, once the vows have been spoken......

VOWS?! Wait! What about the Von Trapps?!!! Cliiiiiiiiimb every mountain!!! I must live the life I was born to live!!!!!

Lisa, dear?

I gotta go!

She presses my hand in hers.
Oh, neat, wow! Groovy laminated card! And Perpetua is my second favorite! Gushing forced appreciation, I genuflect my goodbye.

Heading blessedly out of the convent walls and stepping onto the familiar red brick sidewalk of State Street, the majestic opening chords of JESUS CHRIST

SUPERSTAR resounding in my head, I gulp fresh air and gasp with the sweet scent of a near miss. It's only 2:30 in the afternoon but I head down to THREE DOLLAR DEWEY'S on Fore Street. I'll study the script later. I need to raise a glass and knock one back for Saint Ignatius.

Fishwife

They at Jeffreys today, Lisa?

Yeah, I think so.

Passing the bait wharf around 6pm, the harbormaster calls to me.

Right snotty out theah today, hon!

Yeah, I know.

He shakes his head, shrugs and waves over his shoulder. I clump up the stairs of the iconic footbridge of Perkins Cove in my Helly Hansen rain jacket.

Arrgh! Can you JUST.....?

The northeast wind tears my sou'wester off. Again. I wrassle it back on and stuff it down on my head. At mid-bridge I stop, clutch the seaward rail and stare fruitlessly into the driving wind and darkness. No running lights. No boats. How many nights do I do this?

Fuckin A, TOOOOOODDDDDD!!!!!!! I HATE tub trawling! 25 miles offshore, really? Jeffreys Ledge?! Great offshore fishing grounds but, in February??!!! I know we have no money and you love this life but, DO YOU KNOW WHAT IT IS LIKE TO WAIT FOR YOU ONSHORE NIGHT AFTER NIGHT??!!!!! This, though, is our unspoken bargain: Todd will fish, Lisa will act. And we shall be happy paupers evermore.

Tub trawling or long lining is a type of fishing you can do in pretty much all weathers - unlike lobstering where a steady rail to balance traps is somewhat helpful. Gangions are attached at routine intervals to hundreds of feet of weighted line with baited hooks on each. Just baiting every night takes hours. Each hundred feet is coiled into a "tub" to be fed out over the stern to sit on the bottom overnight and catch fish. Yeah, catching fish would be the point. This particular type of fishing is somewhat "fish friendly" as you typically catch only your target fish - no by-catch that must be discarded and killed for nothing. Well, it's "fish friendly" if you're not a cusk.

All lines on boats are potentially dangerous. There is a reason any seasoned fisherman will advise you to "never ever step on a line". Wrong timing when the line is playing out and your boot with foot attached are in its path and you are going overboard with that line and headed to bottom. Sobering thought, best remembered. A lot can go wrong on a fishing boat.

Leaving at six am daily, seven days a week, Todd and his mate, my brother, Mark, don't return until 6 pm or after. If the weather is bad, which you can be sure it always is in February, they get back much later. This fishing life wears a fishwife down. So, anxiety building, I head to the bridge. Every night I perform this ritual. Must be amusing to the locals. Or heartbreaking - not sure which. I don't have a choice, though. As soon as Todd and Mark get in after a twelve-hour day where they routinely take green water over the bow - that means breaking waves, not just spray - and which warrants risky climbing up forward to chip the weighty ice from the trunk cabin while at cruising speed with hands frozen to their gloves, I truck his load of cusk (a bottom fish similar to cod and just as tasty) to Long Wharf, Portland, Maine and sell the day's catch to dealer, Reggie Graves.

Squinting into the inky black: Okay. Is that them? Weak distant running lights. YES! I recognize the working lights back aft of the FV LIZZIE, as in, Fishing Vessel Lizzie, named for me, steaming past the cans into Perkins Cove. Thank you, Jesus! A gust rips my sou'wester off. That's your son, God - gimme a break, will ya? Breathing regulates. Heart rate, too.
Once at the bait wharf, offloading eight or more boxes - hundreds of pounds of fish - takes another half hour or more.

Mark hollers from the Lizzie up to me where I lurk by the hoist.

Hey, Lizzie! Did ya get WOMEN AND CHILDREN FIRST yet?

The latest Van Halen album. My brother and I are both obsessed with rock and roll.

Yeah, it's pretty great.

Todd now, from on deck:
Hey, Lise, is the truck fueled up?

Yeah, yeah.

When it comes to fishing, Todd pays attention to details. I wait.

Later, after my forty-five minute drive into Portland:

Hey! Lisa! Howyadoin?! Whaddya got, deeah? Whoa! Quite a load today!

Hey, Jake! Yeah, I know. Pretty great, huh?

When I back the old clunker down the aging wharf to Reggie's place, young guys busy with a thousand other boats suddenly forget what they're doing, drop everything and come offload my truck. Handy part of being any female in a man's world. Being twenty something and not what you'd expect getting out of a fish truck helps, too.

Climbing the rickety stairs to get paperwork from the boss I ask:

What's the price today, Reg?

He adjusts his bolo tie accented with a huge turquoise stone and gives me a quote.

Nice!

And, heading back down,
Thanks, guys, see you tomorrow!

Hey! Keep it under ninety, deeeaaahh!!!! Ha, ha!

Making my way down Commercial Street, WBLM blaring out the windows of Todd's rusty Chevy: "we've got to hold on to what we've got, doesn't make a difference if we make it or not....."! Jon Bon Jovi!!!!!!!! LIVING ON A PRAYER! Whatever that is, it is soooooo UUUUSSSSS!!!!!!!!!

Shulamine

"Shulamine" - actually "Charlemagne", but, THEY PRONOUNCE IT
"SHU-LA-MINE", cutthroat French card game, is in full swing at Uncle Roy's
house in Dexter. The cards are hot and the conversation with my French family
is lively. Mom is holding forth with her brothers about their mom, my Mémère,
and the Catholic church. The air is thick with French, their language of origin,
all mashed together with English.

Ohmygod, Father Gautier!!! He was so awful!

Le plus mal!

Big round of guffaws. Uncle Joel spits out some of his beer.

He would glare at us so hard. Then he would announce the passions like we
would be next to suffer. Ha, ha, ha!

Vous allez suffrir les feus d'enfer!

More beer lost.

When we got home from church Mom would say to us, "well, we don't believe
that at all!"

My Mémère must have been referring to the priest's homily of the day. Apparently, my Mémère had a discerning ear when it came to pious men in sketchy robes making dubious proclamations. My mom carries on:

Mom said he wanted to come to the house to bless us - all thirteen of us. I think he was most worried about the boys. And she told him "no, thank you." Ha, ha, ha! She didn't want him in the house!

Roy rocks back in his chair and wheezes his signature laugh with eyes all crinkled and face bright red.

Pas dans la maison!

Jimmy slaps the table and yowls. Mom exclaims:

That damn priest never came!

Il n'a pas ose! Ha, ha, ha!!!!

Another raucous round of hilarity.

Oh, Mom hated that priest; he was so judgmental! Ha, ha!

My mom throws her head back, clutches her breast and catches her breath from laughing and then continues her revelatory tale.

Ha. Ha. HA?! WHAT?! Are you KIDDING me, Mom?! Mémère, MY Mémère, YOUR mom, told you not to believe certain things the priest said?!!!!!!! When you were still young and when it could have made a difference in how much damage the Catholic Church inflicted on you?! WHY DIDN'T YOU TELL ME THE SAME??!!!!!

I have graduated college. I am married and in my twenties when Mom stopped going to church and started recounting untold stories of her childhood about her mom, my Mémère, and priests and prayers and Lent and things not to be believed. What novel demon inhabits my mother's formerly devout body? Unbeknownst to my mom, I have been in counseling with three different therapists for nearly five years but those attempts at unraveling my years of indoctrination by the Catholic Church into its rhetoric of sin has done little to lessen my conviction that I deserve persecution and am bad to the bone. For a woman who doesn't prattle much, she does go on:

Ohmygod, Mom would gather all of us in the kitchen every night of Lent - Lionel, Lucien, Norman, Pat, Orel, Reggie, Roy, Jimmy, Joel, Annette and me - and on our knees we would have to say every damn prayer of that damn rosary. No one could last!

She catches her breath again after another shriekful laugh.....

....it took forever! Ha, Ha, ha!!

Nous etions mourir de rire!

Especially when Orel and Reggie would start to giggle or Jimmy would say he was hungry or when Annette passed out again like she always did. Ha, ha!

Another huge chuckle from my uncles.
She won't stop:

Sometimes Mom would pinch us but she couldn't help herself and then she would laugh, too! Ha, ha! Ohmygod, she was so mad at us but she couldn't stop us!

Wow.

Wow. Wow. Wow. Mom! Must've been nice for Lent to be such a laugh riot for the Laferrieres instead of the long hellish hell of forty days and forty nights without some beloved thing like, say, ice cream or Sunday dessert! Except for that one year when I gave up lime lollipops. I hate lime lollipops. Boy, were you annoyed. I thought it was ingenious - and hilarious. But:
WHYDIDN'TYOUTELLMEYOUNEVERBOUGHTALLTHISCHURCHSHIT??
!!!!!!!!

My Mémère

Oh, no, we are going to go in the hole, Leezaa!

Mémère, holding her cards against her chest and shaking her head as I push the bidding up past 56.

Uncle Roy, as always, takes the bait - he'd bid on absolutely nothing but one King and no suit in his hand, luck out, hit the kitty and his partner like magic and make 63 instantly if not Game. Roy's a crazy bidder. He's playing with Todd right now and we are having a typical cutthroat evening of a favorite card game in my French family called "63". It's a four-person game and there are more of us than that but, no matter, uncles and aunts join in the fun by egging people on while hinting at cards in various players' hands - wildly illegal but it goes on anyway - and shaking their heads at over-the-top bids and missed opportunities. Mémère's salted Spanish peanuts and Canada mints, both white and pink, sit nearby in cozy heaping bowls. The pinks are my favorite. No one drinks although my French uncles do love their beer on occasion. It is always like this when Todd and I descend for a weekend away from Orono on my Mémère's elder housing unit in Dexter, Maine with our two cats, Sassafrass and Dark Star: word gets out quickly and all four of my mother's nine brothers and my aunts who live in Dexter start coming by to see us and tell stories, ask us everything about Orono and us and, importantly, play cards.

The cats scatter to the couch in the living room; we play in the tiny kitchen. Mémère is afraid of cats because long ago one jumped on her back while she was dressing and surprised her but, she always wants Todd and I to come. We can't leave the cats for a weekend so we bring them and she tolerates them. I think she kind of likes them. Today my whole gang of aunts and uncles are here: Joel and Sandy, Lionel and Florice, Betty and Jimmy and Roy and Barbara; Mémère loves it. I love it.

Hey, hey! What you doing there, Joel?! You can't do that!

Roy chastises his younger brother.

Joel: What you mean " I can't do that? Why not? I have no suit; I can play junk!

Roy: You can't play junk when I led with clubs and you have a a club in your hand!

My uncles' thick French accents color their speech; it is such a familiar sound. The teasing is nonstop. Roy to Joel:

C'est comme ca qu'on jouer le jeu!

And Mémère, with fire:
C'est comme ca qu'on va perde tout!

French and English are always flying around the table. I have the equivalent of five years of high school French and have grown up listening to this language but, sadly, was not forced to speak. So, I understand a lot but am shy to try out my own French. Everyone talks over everyone else and we laugh all the time. I love my huge French family. I love my extended Greek family. Family is something this tamed rebel has melted into her core. Growing up with three languages and cultures in our house is something I think everyone experiences until I find out that's not the case and how lucky I am to have this cultural richness as well as unconditional love.

When you going to come again, Leeza?

Mémère in broken English, wishing always we could stay longer.

Maybe in a week or two, Mémère, okay? I love you!

In the cold morning air she waves and waves and I do, too, until we round the bend and are out of sight.

Mémère is the grandparent who I know best. And not just because after several strokes she lived with us when I was in school, but really because of this hanging out we do when I am grown up and on my own. She talks to me and tells me things she has never told me before - sometimes things I wonder if she has told anyone before. I can talk to her in a way I couldn't with my mom; grandmothers and granddaughters luck out there. I want her to live forever.

Your Mother Should Know

I don't feel good. I wish Mom was here.
Hacking coughing fit.

Crap!!!!!! I had a runny nose on New Year's Day and now that means I will be getting sick all year.

"Whatever you do on New Year's Day you will do all year long."

God. Is that one French or Greek? I get them mixed up. Oh, of course, it's French.

MOM!!!!!! Why did you curse us with this stupid superstition for the first day of every year??!!!!! I nearly dislocate my arm while reaching for random forestry products to ward off perceived threats, the pile of salt behind my left shoulder could treat the Northeast corridor all winter long and, saddest of all, I never compliment a loved one on their attractiveness lest capricious evil spirits intervene!

GOD. MOM!!!!!!!!!! Dad!!!!!! Greek family! French family! GEEZ!!!!!
And, don't get me started on the host of nautical and theatrical superstitions embedded in my psyche but, could you get those bananas off this boat! And, man, if you whistle backstage, you'd better LOOK OUT for an errant falling fresnel!

My feverish brain won't stop, though:

"Sing at the table, cry before bedtime." French?

"If someone compliments you or your loved one, you must spit three times - preferably on them - to ward off the evil eye".
Definitely gotta be Greek.

"Wear a new item on Saturday and have another before it wears out!"
French? Greek? In my delirium I can't remember; there are so many superstitions in my family I get them mixed up even when my brain hasn't been fried to mush by a virus.

Chin chin! But you'd better look me in the eye!

Argghh. Hack, hack! Eighth day into a 104 degree fever with bronchitis again and all I want is Mom's cool hand on my forehead, her reassuring voice and healing spirit. Mom is a natural born healer. A psychic once told her she was a very important doctor in China many lifetimes ago and none of us find this hard to believe. It is not just her ancient remedies, it is herself, her person who heals. Yeah, she's got her superstitions - both sides of the family have that up the ying-yang - but, she is also a healer.

We don't fight anymore, Mom and I, or, at least not much. When we do it does still tend to be biblical. But no one has been sacrificed on an altar yet. I know my mom has my back in a way no one else ever can. She's my mom. She has been my champion and my foil. I know now she was strict because she saw the wildness in me. And, the fear. We didn't know how to coexist when I was a teen and sometimes it's still hard because we are so different but similar, too. She protects me. I protect her. Good luck really knowing each other with that agenda. Now that we do not live together I can see her and she me.

Coughing fit.

I will never get over wishing I had my mom when I am sick or when life has gotten too much. Her love of life, her joy, her ardent belief that life will get better and "somehow or other the sun will rise" rubs off on me, turns me around and makes the darkness - my constant companion - just a bit more bearable.

Hi, Mom.

I croak this out over the phone.

You're sick!

Yeah.

Do you have avgolemono?

(Greek chicken, egg and lemon soup that heals all things that need healing - or, we wish.)

Can Todd make it for you?

Yes, yes, Mom, he will. I'm not hungry.

I want you to take ginger, honey and lemon and follow that with a ponge (French hot drink of ginger, milk and honey). Have you taken your temperature?

Yes, Mom. 104.

Well, we need to get that down. Drink two glasses of water and call me back. And get Todd to make you that soup.

Okay, Mom, thanks.

Back on Court Street in Bangor, Maine, I click the receiver into its comfortable Bakelite cradle. Mom's healing powers aided by the miracle of AT&T. Hey, thanks, Alexander G. Good luck with those antitrust laws. I'm sure it'll all work out for ya!

I'm gonna get better now; I just know it.

I love you so much, Mom. I really do.

Made.

I am finally "me".

Whatever that is, you will always know. But, here's the thing: if you don't know, don't "get" me? I don't care.

LIAR!!!!!!!

Okay, I care. A little. But, not like I did. Because, like I said, I am now "in my bones"; I am okay with being me. It doesn't mean I am done growing or don't want to change because I always want to do both. It means I do not need anyone to affirm me. I need no one to confirm my reality just as no one should seek my confirmation for theirs. I do not know anymore what it means to be anything but authentically me - in the moment, vivid, truthful and real. And sometimes, really friggin' pissed! At pretty much EVERYTHING. But, also, I am kind. I am generous. I am honest and I work hard at being a better person all the time. I try to learn from my mistakes; I admit when I'm wrong.

Even though I hate being right all the time.

I am still uncomfortable here. I think humans have "had their shot" and it is time for some wiser beings to emerge and make this planet a better place.

And, God? Goddesses? Whatever you are if you are? I'll keep you in mind as a possibility. I think if you are what people think you are, you're unconditional, boundless love. Your religions with your gated communities can hang onto your keycards.

Whoa!

CLANG!

That's it. The Forever Hippie Garden gate is shut. Maybe that "forgiveness" thing will help me out in a pinch.

Dropping anchor in Virgin Gorda, British Virgin Islands, Todd convinces me and I finally agree to it. A feeling of weight descends; it feels portentous. I don't know what I feel spiritually anymore. Quantum physics - so reminiscent of Eastern mysticism - seems infinitely comforting and cozy. Reincarnation has always been most plausible to me and, because of that, I have never shaken the feeling that, karmically, I need to become a mom in order to finally get the hell out of here for good. "Here" being Earth. And, I kinda have always wanted to be one.

We've sailed a long way to get here. Sigh. The Caribbean sunset is exquisite; the balmy evening air sultry and sexy and we are in love. Here we go.

It's a girl!

Oh, God. Oh, Goddesses! I never cared about the sex of my child. Healthy is all I ever wanted. My firstborn is a GIRL?? Yikes. Mom and I used to fight a lot. They place her on my chest and these thoughts evaporate. I feel every cell in my body - like some big, organic clockworks - shift their cogs in a kind of alchemic and permanent realignment. Kafka comes to mind. Six legs, exoskeleton not emerging though. My chrysalis is torn open. Two births today. I wear my organs on the outside from now on; there is a little person I care for more than anyone before in my life. There is no "I". There is only "her". I stare in awe at this tiny girl in my arms. This love is fierce, exhilarating, terrifying, inexorable.

What's her name? Who is she?

She's...Gelsey. Her name is Gelsey. She'll let me know who she is.

Her penetrating almond eyes look up darkly and suspiciously into mine:

MAKE ME.

Oh, God. Uh oh.

Now my - I mean, OUR - new journey begins.

Acknowledgements

My abounding gratitude to my beloved sister, Karen, for line-editing, encouragement, everlasting support, surpassing love and for being my beloved sister "without whom I would never survive", to my good friend and fellow writer, Valerie Kuhn Reid for being a first and avid reader and making her wise and valuable critiques. To William (Bill) Steele[1] for his enthusiasm and sage counsel, to Jackie Reifer[2], extraordinary performer and creator, for being such a kind advisor and advocate and just a plain joy to know. To Mary Snell[3], most excellent writer, theatre critic and incisive reader who provided much-needed guidance to make the narrative clearer. Megan Grumbling[4], beautiful poet and theatrically wise reviewer for her longtime support. To Karlyn Daigle[5], my beloved Sound Engineer, for her "sound advice" and whose extraordinary talent has always helped me deliver my best audio performance. To my beloved lifelong friend, Janet O'Donnell, for putting me on stage and leading me to a life in the theater. And to my cherished colleague, Michael Rafkin[6], for his faith, appreciation and long friendship as well as for all of our years together as kindred theatre artists. And, to michael: beautiful artist and patient collaborator every step of the way with MAKE ME, for being my partner and my love.

And lastly, to my surpassingly brilliant editor as well as my best friend of nearly forty years, Suze Allen, for her exacting and scrupulous editing, her uncanny ability to "see" the shape of the entire story, her pitch perfect notes and for her endless love. She is largely to blame for my writing this book and I thank her for challenging me and urging me on my journey and insisting that I write on and on. Love forever.

[1]Bill Steele, Professor of Theater at USM from 1967 through 2016, former drama critic for the Portland Press Herald and author of four books on theater and film, including "Stay Home and Star: A Step-by-Step Guide to Starting Your Regional Acting Career" and "Acting in Industrials: The Business of Acting for Business"

[2]Jackie Reifer, comedienne, mime, speech & language therapist, and touring member with Tony Montanaro's Celebration Theater Ensemble.

[3]Mary Snell, MFA -- writer and poet; former staff writer and theater critic, Maine Sunday Telegram; awarded Kennedy Center Medallion (via Critics' Institute of American College Theater Festival); former Maine Arts Commission jury panelist; founded Hellenic Society of Maine and USM/Aegean Arts & Cultural Exchange with Republic of Greece.

[4]Megan Grumbling, Megan writes poetry, criticism and essays, and dramatic works, and serves as an editor, teacher, and writing mentor. Her second poetry collection, "Persephone in the Late Anthropocene", is forthcoming in fall of 2020 from Acre Books. Her first collection, "Booker's Point" (UNT 2016), was awarded the Vassar Miller Prize and the Maine Book Award for Poetry. Her work has been awarded the Poetry Foundation's Ruth Lilly Fellowship, the Robert Frost Award from the Robert Frost Foundation, a Hawthornden Fellowship at Hawthornden Castle, Scotland, and a St. Boltoph Emerging Artist Award, and has been included in Best of the Net, Best New Poets, the New York Times Poetry Pairing Series, and Verse Daily.

[5]Karlyn Daigle, audio producer and sound designer. Production Manager, Gaslit Nation. Producer/Engineer, soundbath. Lead sound designer for Wondery's 'Sight Unseen' (2018 Mark Time Gold Award Winner). Co-composer for theme music and various sound beds for Wondery's 'Sight Unseen'. Lead sound designer for Wondery's 'The Dark Tome' podcast (ep. 7 and 8). Engineer for Audible's 'The Starling Project' (2016 Audie Winner). Creator and co-producer of web series Symphony With A Stranger, a promotional effort with Portland Symphony Orchestra.

[6]Michael Rafkin, founding Artistic Director, Mad Horse Theatre, Portland Maine

Songs

Space Oddity
Written by: David Bowie
Lyrics © T.R.O. Inc.

Losing My Religion
Written by: William Thomas Berry, Peter Lawrence Buck, Michael E. Mills,
John Michael Stipe
Lyrics © Universal Music Publishing Group

Dream On
Written by: Steven Victor Tallarico
Lyrics © BMG Rights Management

Levon
Written by: Bernie Taupin, Elton John
Lyrics © Universal Music Publishing Group

Burn Down The Mission
Written by: Bernie Taupin, Elton John
Lyrics © Universal Music Publishing Group

Living In The Past
Written by: Ian Anderson
Lyrics © BMG Rights Management

The Bitch Is Back
Written by: Bernie Taupin, Elton John
Lyrics © Universal Music Publishing Group

Tomorrow Never Knows
Written by: John Lennon, Paul McCartney
Lyrics © Sony/ATV Music Publishing LLC

Drift Away
Written by: Mentor R. Williams
Lyrics © Universal Music Publishing Group

Born To Be Wild
Written by: Mars Bonfire
Lyrics © Universal Music Publishing Group

Crimson And Clover
Written by: Peter Lucia, Tommy James
Lyrics © Sony/ATV Music Publishing LLC

A Hard Day's Night
Written by: John Lennon, Paul McCartney
Lyrics © Sony/ATV Music Publishing LLC, Kobalt Music Publishing Ltd.

Jet
Written by: Linda McCartney, Paul McCartney
Lyrics © Kobalt Music Publishing Ltd.

Doo Doo Doo Doo Doo (Heartbreaker)
Written by: Keith Richards, Mick Jagger
Lyrics © Sony/ATV Music Publishing LLC

Dancing With Mr. D
Written by: Keith Richards, Mick Jagger
Lyrics © Sony/ATV Music Publishing LLC

Get Down Tonight
Written by: Harry Casey, Richard Finch
Lyrics © Sony/ATV Music Publishing LLC

Make Me

You Wreck Me
Written by: Michael W Campbell, Thomas Earl Petty
Lyrics © Gone Gator Music, Warner Chappell Music, Inc.

Won't Get Fooled Again
Written by: Peter Townshend
Lyrics © Spirit Music Group

Voodoo Child (Slight Return)
Written by: Jimi Hendrix
Lyrics © Sony/ATV Music Publishing LLC

Let's Dance
Written by: David Bowie
Lyrics © Tintoretto Music, Sony/ATV Music Publishing LLC

Burning Down The House
Written by: David Byrne, Tina Weymouth, Chris Frantz, Jerry Harrison
Lyrics © Warner Chappell Music, Inc.
I Don't Care Anymore
Written by: Phil Collins
Lyrics © Cocord Music Publishing LLC

I Wouldn't Want To Be Like You
Written by: Alan Parsons, Eric Woolfson
Lyrics © Universal Music Publishing Group

Some Enchanted Evening
Written by: Oscar Hammerstein II, R. Rodgers
Lyrics © Concord Music Publishing LLC

Would I Lie To You
Written by: Annie Lennox, David Allan Stewart
Lyrics © Universal Music Publishing Group, Sony/ATV Music Publishing
LLC

Albums

Neil Young, Harvest
Reprise Records, February 1972

Led Zeppelin, Led Zeppelin IV
Atlantic Records, November 1971

Big Brother and The Holding Company, Cheap Thrills
Columbia Records, August 1968

The Rolling Stones, Let It Bleed
London Recordings, December 1969

Cream, Disraeli Gears
Atlantic Records, November 1967

Led Zeppelin, Led Zeppelin II
Atlantic Records, October 1969

Deep Purple, Made In Japan
Warner Records, December 1972

Herb Alpert & The Tijuana Brass, The Lonely Bull
A&M, December 1962

Van Halen, Women and Children First
Warner Brothers, March 1980

Author

Lisa Stathoplos is an actor, voice artist and special education teacher/behavior specialist. She has been acting on stage, in film and video for forty years and teaching for twenty. Highlights of Lisa's work on stage include Maire in Friel's TRANSLATIONS at Worcester Forum. She was a Spotlight Award nominee for creating the role of Marie in Mike Kimball's THE SECRET OF COMEDY for NY Theater Company, Portsmouth, N.H. She won critical acclaim playing Maria Callas in Terrence McNally's MASTER CLASS at Good Theater. At Portland Stage, she created the role of Marie in Monica Wood's PAPERMAKER and played Sharon in Jen Silverman's THE ROOMMATE. She is a founding member of Mad Horse Theatre Company, Portland. She performed with Eve Ensler in her VAGINA MONOLOGUES at Merrill Auditorium, Portland. Her work as the character of Violet Weston in Tracy Lett's AUGUST:OSAGE COUNTY at Good Theater earned her the 2011 Portland PEER Award for Best Performance.

Film work includes Ellie Lee's DOG DAYS, Winner, Best Short 2000 Hamptons and Florida Film Festivals, FAMILY TREES by Lars Trodson, Berlin Film Festival, Louis Frederick's DRINK ME and her first speaking role on film with a dog returned from the dead in Stephen King's PET SEMATARY.

Voice work with PocketUniverse Productions for Audible.com includes voicing Nina Locke in Joe Hill's LOCKE AND KEY/ multiple AUDIE Award winner, Diana Fowley in THE X-FILES, COLD CASES with David Duchovny and Gillian Anderson/2018 multiple AUDIE Award nominee, THE STARLING PROJECT by Jefferey Deavers playing opposite Alfred Molina/2016 AUDIE Award, Best Original Work, THE VAULT OF HORROR from EC Comics/Winner Best AudioDrama, 2020 Independent Book Awards. She played Captain Frey in HOMEFRONT: EXPEDITIONARY FORCE with Kate Mulgrew and Zachary Quinto and won a 2019 Earphones Award/Audiofile Magazine for her narration of Mary Gabriel's NINTH STREET WOMEN.

Lisa moved north from her beloved theatrical home, Portland, Maine, and lives in Searsport with michael and a motley collection of adopted furry creatures.

Editor

Suze Allen is an author, playwright, copy writer, editor, writing coach, dramaturg, teacher and ghost writer. She coauthored THE TIME-STARVED WOMAN'S GUIDE TO EMOTIONAL WELLBEING – TOOLS & STRATEGIES FOR BALANCE with S.D. Shanti M.P.H., PhD and Gabriella Dixson's cookbook, WE LOVE THEM AND WE FEED THEM and was a writer for MINDFUL MOTHERHOOD by Cassandra Vieten PhD, as well as working on a chapter in Marty Selman PhD's book, EXECUTIVE STAMINA. Suze's plays have been produced all over the United States and in Scotland. She served as the Bay Area Regional Rep for The Dramatists Guild of America for 7 years, Resident Dramaturg for 3Girls Theatre, which she also co-founded, and for The Playwrights' Center of SF, where she also taught playwriting. She has written marketing and website copy for hundreds of clients, and created and edited newsletters for Mama's Resource Network and many other organizations. Suze also writes articles on spec for companies like sfkids and Interaction Associates. She teaches online classes in memoir writing, playwriting and writing through grief. www.manuscriptmentor.com

Book Designer and Cover Artist

Michael Crockett is a father and retired educator as well as a visual artist, actor, director, playwright, set designer, web designer, and self-publishing consultant. A native of Portland, Maine, he now shares his life in the midcoast with lisa, two dogs and five cats.

CPSIA information can be obtained
at www.ICGtesting.com
Printed in the USA
LVHW111528260321
682579LV00008B/47/J

9 781647 194215